Artificial Intelligence in Schools

Artificial Intelligence in Schools is the first book to explore the use of Artificial Intelligence (AI) as a tool to enhance K–12 instruction and administration. Every industry and sector will be drastically affected by the presence of artificial intelligence, and schooling is no exception! Written for the in-service community—leaders, administrators, coaches, and teachers alike—this is your one-stop opportunity to make sure you don't fall behind the fast pace and promising innovations of today's most advanced learning technology. Author Varun Arora presents AI as a problem-solving tool for teaching and learning, exploring its potential and application in real-world school contexts and in the language of educators. Covering curriculum development, feedback and scoring, student empowerment, behavioral and classroom management, college readiness, and more, the book is full of novel insights and concrete, strategic takeaways.

Varun Arora is CEO of OpenCurriculum, an education technology company that uses expert systems, natural language processing technologies, and knowledge on effective instructional practices to help K–12 teachers design high-quality curriculum and instruction using research and evidence from classrooms around the world.

Other Eye On Education Books
Available From Routledge
(www.routledge.com/k-12)

**Thriving as an Online K-12 Educator:
Essential Practices from the Field**
Jody Peerless Green

**Coding as a Playground:
Programming and Computational Thinking in the
Early Childhood Classroom**
Marina Umaschi Bers

**Making Technology Work in Schools:
How PK-12 Educators Can Foster Digital-Age Learning**
Timothy D. Green, Loretta C. Donovan, and
Jody Peerless Green

**Integrating Computer Science Across the Core:
Strategies for K-12 Districts**
Tom Liam Lynch, Gerald Ardito, and Pam Amendola

**The Genius Hour Guidebook:
Fostering Passion, Wonder, and
Inquiry in the Classroom**
Denise Krebs and Gallit Zvi

**Tech Request: A Guide for Coaching
Educators in the Digital World**
Emily L. Davis and Brad Currie

Artificial Intelligence in Schools

A Guide for Teachers, Administrators, and Technology Leaders

Varun Arora

NEW YORK AND LONDON

Cover design by Varun Arora, with contributions by Alexander R. Wilcox Cheek and Jenessa Peterson.

First published 2022
by Routledge
605 Third Avenue, New York, NY 10158

and by Routledge
4 Park Square, Milton Park, Abingdon, Oxon, OX14 4RN

Routledge is an imprint of the Taylor & Francis Group, an informa business

© 2022 Varun Arora

The right of Varun Arora to be identified as author of this work has been asserted in accordance with sections 77 and 78 of the Copyright, Designs and Patents Act 1988.

All rights reserved. No part of this book may be reprinted or reproduced or utilised in any form or by any electronic, mechanical, or other means, now known or hereafter invented, including photocopying and recording, or in any information storage or retrieval system, without permission in writing from the publishers.

Trademark notice: Product or corporate names may be trademarks or registered trademarks, and are used only for identification and explanation without intent to infringe.

Library of Congress Cataloging-in-Publication Data
A catalog record for this title has been requested

ISBN: 978-1-03-202399-1 (hbk)
ISBN: 978-1-03-200905-6 (pbk)
ISBN: 978-1-00-318323-5 (ebk)

DOI: 10.4324/9781003183235

Typeset in Palatino
by Newgen Publishing UK

Dedicated to teachers throughout the world who come to school tirelessly every day and work harder than any machine, with the singular goal of changing the lives of our students.

Contents

Acknowledgments xi
Foreword. xiii
Preface xvii

1 Introduction: Where We Are Today. 1
  Brief highlights of how much progress AI has made so far, in the context of teacher workload.
  Intro to pattern recognition, making predictions, models, neural networks, and more.

2 Feedback and Scoring. 27
  Correcting assignments and giving feedback faster
  Intro to convolutional neural networks, recurrent neural networks, image recognition, natural language processing, and more.

3 Improving College Readiness. 53
  How to find the ones who we are leaving behind.
  Intro to classification, clustering, machine translation, and more.

4 Empowering Students With Physical and Learning Challenges 71
  Understanding and giving students with challenges new ways to express themselves.
  Intro to natural language generation, syntax parsing, conversational modeling, entities, question-answer systems, artificial general intelligence, and more.

5   **Behavior and Classroom Management** 93
    Capturing behavior and classroom management
       issues before they happen.
    *Intro to computer vision, facial recognition, affect detection,
       Markov models, learning analytics, and more.*

6   **Curriculum Development and Alignment** 113
    Building teaching and learning experiences
       and materials.
    *Intro to knowledge extraction and representation, knowledge
       components, expert systems, knowledge tracing, student
       modeling, summarization, interpretability, comprehension,
       common sense understanding, generative adversarial
       networks, and more.*

7   **Deeper, Higher-order, Authentic Learning** 147
    Moving away from rote-learning-driven
       curriculum to deeper learning.
    *Intro to TF-IDF, n-grams, topic discovery, Markov decision
       processes, reinforcement learning, human-in-the-loop,
       recommender systems, intelligence augmentation,
       and more.*

8   **Teacher Education and Professional Development** 165
    Supporting relevant teacher learning.
    *Intro to misconception analysis, word2vec, virtual
       reality, imitation learning, and more.*

9   **Challenges** 177
    Why doing many of the things in previous chapters
       is still hard, and what we need to get around those
       issues.
    Lack of Enough Data
    Data, data, everywhere, but no data to train with.

Accuracy
It works most times, but is that enough?

Domain-specific Research
It works elsewhere, but not in the classroom. Yet.

10 Getting Started With Making New AI Innovations ...191
Caught some AI feels? Keep these big ideas in mind as you begin to bring something new to life.

11 Future 203
Where we are going and how we can succeed collectively, and why optimism should be our best friend.

Appendix A: A Short History of AI For Improving
   Teaching and Learning..............................207
Appendix B: Common Natural Things Turned to
   Mathematical Data.................................219
Index..230

Acknowledgments

This book would not be possible without rounds of inputs and advice by the following people, in no particular order: Lingqi Zhang (San Mateo County Office of Education), Pualani Smith (Grade 1 teacher), Anirudh Koul (Head of R&D, Aira and founder of Microsoft Seeing AI), Marjorie Carlson (former Carnegie Mellon University Academic coach and Google Engineer), Shayan Doroudi (Asst. Professor of Education, UC Irvine), Pradyumna Tambwekar (PhD candidate in Machine Learning at Georgia Tech University), Brandon Dorman (Lead Assessment Specialist and IMS Global CASE WorkGroup Co-Chair and former middle and high-school mathematics teacher), Markus Kliegl (Research Engineer at DeepMind), Robert Murphy (RAND Corporation), Elijah Mayfield (former VP of TurnItIn), Bena Kallick (co-founder of Institute for Habits of Mind), Cecilia Zhao (G2 Capital), Greg Diamos (Senior Research Scientist), Shadi Yazdan (former K-8 teacher and trainer in Ontario, Canada), Fahim Dalvi (Qatar Computing Research Institute), Priyank Sharma (PhD candidate in Education), Neha Jacob (BDO), Samreen Anjum (PhD candidate in Information Sciences at UT Austin), Jessica Dickinson Goodman (Social Justice and Tech Facilitator, Foothill College), and Jenessa Peterson (Director of Learning Engineering at The Learning Agency). I am certain that this list is incomplete, so I thank you if you were involved in making this possible.

Also, a big thanks to my parents, my brother, and his wife, for being a constant source of unconditional love and support. I am also very grateful to Daniel Schwartz at my publisher, Routledge (imprint of Taylor & Francis), for believing in me and my vision for this book, and Jen Hinchliffe, for her invaluable edits to make the book more readable and enjoyable.

Lastly, I want to thank you for picking up this book either online or at a physical bookstore. Without your effort in reading this, these are just bunches of thoughts on pieces of paper which have no significance in the world we wish to create for our future generations.

Foreword

I've always been excited by the different ways of using technology to make my life just a little easier in trying to understand and reach my students. But I could never have predicted the ways I'd need to be ready for a sudden shift to an online teaching environment during COVID-19, where I lost full control over the classroom.

I started out teaching mathematics over 30 years ago in schools serving low-to-medium-income populations. For most of the early 1990s, technology resources in these schools were scarce. The only digital technology we used to help kids learn was occasionally rolling out a boxy television set and VCR from the library into the classroom for a documentary video. The school's overhead projectors were locked away most of the time and were only brought out for a couple of annual professional development sessions.

I decided to tutor struggling students in my living room after school. During these early years, photocopying machines and printers were expensive to access. So, to make multiple copies of worksheets of mathematical problems, my wife and I would spend hours at night writing out these worksheets using carbon paper slipped between sheets of normal paper. In a few years, however, we excitedly made the transition to using personal computers and printers. This dramatically reduced the time taken to prepare for classes, and we were easily able to make multiple worksheets with different combinations of mathematical problems. My opportunities to understand students came from checks for understanding in class periods, tutoring sessions, and graded assignments. I never saw these interactions as being limited in any way. But I believed that more time spent on learning was the key to success.

And then, about a decade ago, I moved to teaching at an international school, where more funding and higher school fees meant the presence of smart boards, iPads, and Apple TV's. While my role as a teacher and mentor never changed, I could move around with my iPad in hand to reach my students and sit with them and watch their work get projected on a big screen at the front of the classroom. I was moving one more step away from being a sage-on-the-stage. Students could help each other as they watched their peers' work on the screen.

But the COVID-19 pandemic changed everything, while changing nothing at all. While "share my screen" became one click away for most students, I found it more difficult to see my students' learning. Whether or not I was ready, I, like hundreds of thousands of teachers around the world, could not use the same bag of tricks I did for all these years in gauging if my students were with me as I taught. However, while I had gradually tip-toed my way to making technology support me over several years, most teachers had not built such a cooperative relationship with technology. As I heard from former colleagues and read about schooling around the world, the quality of learning had just taken a big blow. Teaching hadn't moved forward by very much, regardless of technology. In the absence of high-quality teaching, technology was being aimed at filling more and more accessibility voids for families with means, albeit poorly.

I continued to adapt my style as I ran full-length live online lessons. As a parent, however, I saw my youngest child come home with a different educational approach. His school gave him access to an online mathematics learning resource that would help him learn mathematical concepts independently. When he made a mistake on a problem, the computer would give him scaffolded hints and video lessons along the way, no matter how the student solves the problem. It also allowed the teacher to see what grade level the students were at and provided the teacher with a deeper insight into student performance. I learned that this was possible because of Artificial Intelligence (AI), and that

I would be expected to use something like this for students in higher classes as well.

For the first time, while every teacher's work has increased, it may seem like a teacher's role is reducing. And yet, in my opinion, as a large percentage of students continue to struggle around the world, with or without access to technology, the role of a teacher has never been more important. I believe that only a teacher can convincingly explain to a student—while keeping in mind his/her unique learning sensitivity and ability—why they made a specific mistake in a specific situation. Only a teacher can foster a collaborative learning environment where the students can learn from each other. And only a teacher can motivate a student to care. And, so, I felt that as long as I stayed true to doing these things while using the technologies adopted at my school, the idea of AI in education was not something I ever needed to broach in any depth.

And yet, this book changed my mind. I am now convinced that teachers must take a more active role, when it comes to AI, and embrace the opportunity to learn about it a little further, particularly because of how much it impacts our work in student learning. One of the things the author, Varun Arora, succeeds brilliantly at is his ability to get me, an everyday classroom teacher, excited about the idea of AI. The book feels like something akin to a mystery novel where each new concept feels like a clue that solves one problem and takes you a little closer to the bigger answer of the great potential that AI can have on how we can better teach our kids. Varun does a beautiful job of explaining the terminologies that one might face when listening to experts in AI talk about the subject, so that non-expert teachers can be active participants in conversations about it.

This book never reads like a dull textbook. This is because Varun's lived experience has allowed him to have a unique insight into the perspectives of teachers, scientists working with AI, administrators in education who know about the complexities that schools and teachers face, and students themselves.

Varun is sympathetic to, and has a great understanding of, the struggles that teachers face. In a book about technology, I felt seen and recognized. It felt like I was being given the language to explain struggles with teaching that I was never quite able to put into words. And then he went on to provide evidence-based actionable suggestions to overcome these struggles.

Whether you are a teacher, a student, or someone who is simply interested in education, AI, and/or its intersection with education, allow this book to gently introduce you to some complex, yet important ideas that have been explained wonderfully. And if anything piques your interest—I'm certain that something will—let yourself begin exploring these ideas further with the reading suggestions that Varun has helpfully provided. Let your eyes be opened to a whole new fascinating world of the age-old practice of teaching and the wonderful new doors that AI can open. And most of all, enjoy the work of my student, of whose career trajectory I am supremely proud to have been a part.

Sen K. Jose
University of Chicago Outstanding
Educator Award 2020 Winner

Preface

Let us just be honest here for a second, before we get started. I am guessing that you picked this book up because you are the kind of person who cares a lot about education and improving the future for your people. At the same time, pretty much everywhere you go, you hear someone talking on and on about Artificial Intelligence (AI). The guy on your TV is talking about it, the ads on your social media are about it, heck even the old people you know are beginning to say things with "AI" in it. It will "change the future," they say. Many are even saying that it will change education as we know it.

But if you are a teacher, you and your teacher friends have heard phrases like "it will change everything" and "disruption" and "breakthrough" before. They said that about desktop computers, the new textbooks, smart boards, projectors, online quizzes, twenty-first-century skills, the new standards, virtual teaching, and more. Some were easier to figure out than others, but you generally knew what these things were before they entered your classroom.

This time around though, **you feel like you don't know**. Yes, it seems like AI is one of the greatest innovations out there, but despite being as technology-savvy as you are, you can't really tell what this thing is. Some people are even saying that AI might replace teachers—which sounds preposterous, but you don't know how to refute that odd claim. Others are simply saying "AI" when they mean technology in general.

This time is also different because some part of you is tired of schools being handed down technology by wealthy technologists without understanding what you want and what your students are experiencing. This is modern technology tyranny.

This book is all about changing that.

Reading this book will put you in the driver's seat. This book is about helping you understand what AI is, in the context of its potential value in teaching and learning. It will help you to unpack AI successes that are in products all around you. And it will give you the necessary background knowledge to discuss what good AI in teaching and learning in the future could look like. This knowledge will empower you to make informed decisions about the role you may want it to play in your teaching, sooner and more reliably than your peers will figure it out.

To take it one step further, my hope is that the book will help you partner with technology makers to create AI for improving education in the future. I envision a future where educators are not mere recipients of "cool" technologies, which they are forced to retrofit into their teaching process, but rather active shapers of these innovations, because they understand the possibilities of the technology.

In this book, I want to focus on **screen-less** Kindergarten through Grade 12 (henceforth, "K–12") schools. When I say "screen-less," I mean physical brick-and-mortar schools with a teacher in there calling the shots in classrooms. Basically, it is more or less what you think of when we talk about a regular school or a classroom around the world without one-to-one computing for each child. If we didn't know already, the pandemic caused by COVID-19 was a stark reminder of the global challenges in making personal laptops, mobile phones, and stable Internet connectivity available to every student. Even where they were available, we began craving a return to in-person learning in physical schools due to the loss of so many learning opportunities attributable to the limitations of an unsustainable and complex digital world. I also focus specifically on the teaching and learning process. This leaves out many other problems in the larger education space.

But who am I and why should you read anything written by me? I could either be perceived as a teacher in the shoes of a technology creator, or a technology creator with the heart of a teacher. For most of my professional career, I have been working inside and outside the classroom on core curricular and achievement-related problems. The bug to improve quality of learning bit me at any early age. I started tutoring students when I was 14 years old and publishing textbook summaries by the time I was 16. I was then formally trained in solving complex knowledge problems in social contexts, sometimes using technology. I chose this path because I had a hunch that to understand learning, one needed a fundamental understanding of knowledge and information. I later realized that a quintessential requirement of understanding the process of learning is an understanding of how humans interact with knowledge and information.

Along the way, I have taught undergraduates in a university, and then later had a brief stint teaching science experimentation to elementary school students in a public school with a largely non-native student population. I also consulted a Ministry of Education in Polynesia on their policies and infrastructure to support learning equality. In the past decade, however, most of my work has primarily focused on K–12 curriculum quality and teaching improvement, often involving use of the "least-invasive" technologies. And in more recent years, I have worked in one of the most innovative AI research labs in the world, pushing the boundaries of what is possible.

What I Generally Believe About AI in Teaching and Learning

AI, in its broader sense,[1,2] has enormous potential in improving various aspects of teaching and learning. And that is the optimism behind the examples of work I share in this book.

That said, I have a confession before we begin.

Despite my belief in the potential of AI, I am skeptical. In my opinion, AI is **not** going to be a silver bullet in education for a while—at least for a couple of decades. By "not being a silver bullet," I mean it isn't going to be the magic sauce or perfect solution to the achievement problems schools around the world face, unless something radically changes about how schools are organized, funded, and led, and more importantly, unless the AI ecosystem around teaching and learning matures a lot more, something I discuss throughout this book.

To add to that, I believe that during this period, the investments in technology that will give us the highest return in student learning are ones that harness traditional education research, pedagogical content knowledge (the understanding of how to teach specific things), and good product sense. Some people may consider these to be boring and non-sexy things, but when tied with a well-designed school system, leadership, and solid partnerships between technology builders and educators, they can give us great success without needing to depend on a mature AI ecosystem.

That said, we won't have to wait for a couple of decades before we can start reaping benefits from the use of AI. Since AI is not one single application or algorithm, but rather a large set of techniques, individual or combinations of AI techniques may be used as catalysts to deliver better learning outcomes without disrupting the "traditional" learning process today.

Don't feel afraid of these complicated techniques; we will discuss many of them, one by one, in ways that will make you feel like you are reading a story with key details. Sometimes there is going to be some mathematical terminology involved. If you are worried about being overwhelmed by complicated mathematical terminology, don't be—I'll explain everything as we go along. I was never a mathematics wiz in school, but with the help of some decent teachers and explanations outside a classroom, I was able to make sense of these techniques. And so can you.

Who This Book Is For

This book is primarily for two groups of people: **educators** (teachers, administration, coaches, instructional designers, coordinators in schools, etc.) AND **builders of educational technology**. I think most other people interested in the topic will benefit quite a bit from this read, but I am targeting those who obsessively think about teaching and learning every day.

Additionally, while I am going to primarily be discussing ideas in the context of **K–12 education**, nothing stops you from using these ideas in the higher education context. The key theoretical elements of teaching and learning in education are universal. My mother teaches at a college level, but sometimes her students' skills are at proficiency levels of middle schoolers. Very often, instructional theory targeted at K–12 students works well in her day-to-day practice. I have taught in both settings too, and I can confirm that.

What This Book Is NOT About

I want to be clear here. This book is not:

1. An AI-building tutorial, summary, or review.
2. A guide on how to teach AI to students.
3. A market analysis of AI technologies in education.
4. Written with the highest degree of scientific discipline and accuracy. There are several places where ease of understanding has taken precedence over scientific precision and nuance.
5. A literature review of AI research in education over the past few decades.
6. A guide to becoming a more tech-savvy teacher.

It is, to be honest, **a mile wide and an inch deep**. It is going to let you see an overview of the landscape, but you would need to go somewhere else to get deeper into the minute details—material that is much more widely available these days, including, but not limited to, the references cited in this book. I will try to make it easy for you to know what to search for if you wish to investigate the underlying technologies that AI tools are, and will be made of, in case you are more curious. And thus, this is **a starting point**.

The book isn't going to give you shortcuts and starter packs and downloadable apps on how to use AI in your classroom. AI may merely be seen as a means to achieving a learning goal that you are targeting for your students. If you focus on using AI in the classroom, irrespective of how well it serves the learning goal, it might weaken the quality of learning that you may have been able to facilitate without the use of AI.

If reading about the possibilities in scientific progress in AI pushes you to think of innovative new solutions for education, you would need to go out and seek technical people who can bring these new AI-supported technologies to life. Especially in the form of products that you can share with the community. I absolutely encourage that.

There is another thing I wish to clarify. You may have heard of **Intelligent Tutoring Systems** (ITSs)[3] before. In case you haven't, in short, these are computer programs that engage students in exercises and new material, all while providing custom feedback and taking them through learning pathways that individually adapt to them. A lot of conversations, research,[4] and thorough analysis of AI in education revolves around *ITSs* and adaptive learning applications like online testing tools, and "Massive Open Online Courses" (MOOCs). All of these, anchored by *ITSs*, have given us some of the most important foundational ideas around how computers can begin to understand and reason, based on student learning needs. They have done a lot in allowing us to test our ideas about improving learning, and the intents and efforts of people who have worked on these for so long are very admirable.

Instead of directly focusing on adaptive one-computer-to-one-student learning, I draw on methods and findings from these fields of study and try to use them in the context of *screen-less* classroom environments. I understand that educators' and parents' apprehension about AI in teaching and learning comes primarily from computers taking over the teaching process. This isn't necessarily the intention of the work done in adaptive learning, but some ill-founded applications of adaptive learning methods have spread this narrative. The intention was never to remove the teacher from the equation or dehumanize the process. AI, today, is incapable of making decisions that are anything larger than granular. Taking away a highly superior cognitive planner, that is, the teacher, from the picture makes the entire process ineffective. I, too, have a deep, genuine, and scientific appreciation for the role teachers play.

All too often, the discussion of teacher-led vs computer-led teaching is a touchy-feely or don't-take-away-teacher-jobs one. These are unproductive discussions in the process of finding the best answers for our students and society at large. By focusing on *screen-less* classrooms, where the teacher is still in charge, we can explore the best that AI has to offer, without getting carried away in implications of workforce overhaul.

I don't just say that to keep you distracted from the implications of technology in teaching for the rest of the book. My honest opinion on the future of AI and the education workforce couldn't be further from someone's first guess about the views of an author of a book on AI in schools; I have a strong conviction that teaching is going to be the number one profession of the future. I have not a single doubt that there will be a large need for humans who work closely with, and care for, fewer learners of all ages to understand their needs, aspirations, dilemmas, goals, and feelings and hold them accountable to success, all while utilizing technology and instilling wisdom. Unsurprisingly, we already have a name for such humans; we call them teachers. To ensure we can meet this demand for teachers, the rest of the world will need to work extra-hard to create environments that allow the profession to prosper.

One final thing. As mentioned earlier, this book is focused specifically on **teaching and learning**. Education is a far-wider field of cross-disciplinary study, and geographically contextualized, and I couldn't possibly do justice to many of those problems. And so, I leave out key processes like enrollment, public policy, access, school leadership, accountability, economics/budgets, etc. from these discussions. Plus, explaining AI in the context of taxation of housing in American neighborhoods as it relates to school funding is going to make no sense to an educator in Guatemala, and I don't wish to geographically limit who can make use of this guide.

The focus of this book is to unpack some of the key AI techniques that make up the broad AI applications that are, and will be, accessible to educators in the future. It is not centered around information about applications that have been popular in recent times. I believe that knowing these AI techniques is important because without knowing their details, one cannot effectively argue for what is needed and what is harmful.

Now, at this point, if you do not feel a need to dive into these techniques, and would rather prefer a more general understanding on AI in education, what has been going on in this field for the past couple of decades, its broad implications, and overviews of *Intelligent Tutoring Systems*, consider reading one or more of the following:

- **Intelligence Unleashed: An argument for AI in Education** by Rose Luckin and Wayne Holmes of the UCL Knowledge Lab, University College London and Mark Griffiths and Laurie B. Forcier of Pearson
- **The Impact of Artificial Intelligence on Learning, Teaching, and Education: Policies for the Future** by Ilkka Tuomi, European Commission

- **Artificial Intelligence In Education: Promises and Implications for Teaching and Learning** by Charles Fadel, Wayne Holmes, and Maya Bialik
- **Artificial Intelligence Applications to Support K–12 Teachers and Teaching: A Review of Promising Applications, Opportunities, and Challenges** by Robert F. Murphy, RAND Corporation

How This Book Is Organized

It is pretty straightforward. After the Introduction in Chapter 1, Chapters 2 through 8 highlight, one by one, seven **complex problem spaces** in teaching and learning.

These are neither exclusive, nor are they the most important seven. They are just seven strategically chosen topics that allow me to try to introduce key ideas in AI that form a cohesive set of tools that could be used on teaching and learning problems (as of early 2019). Since the ideas in AI build on top of each other, chapter-over-chapter, this is not really a choose-your-own-adventure or jump-to-any-point book. You need to go in sequence unless you already know a significant amount about AI. Generally, I am going to introduce simpler ideas first, and lead up to more complex ideas after identifying the inadequacies of the simpler things.

In these chapters, I talk about the problems from a very general teaching and learning perspective in paragraphs like this one.

New vocabulary	But often I need to introduce the technology and some mathematical and statistical ideas, and so I put them in boxes like these. These are essential to you learning from this book, so skipping over them will leave you confused in the sections ahead.
They might make you uncomfortable, and you would be keen to skim through them without absorbing the ideas. But a lot of the magic of the book lies in these boxes. So, try to resist the temptation to jump ahead, and try to stay put through the productive struggle process of understanding the content in these boxes.

Tool to try	I occasionally introduce existing tools that are ready for you as a user to try out. These are tools that draw on the key technological ideas and/or problems of the chapters. These tool names come with a simple $ meter, to give you some idea of how much the tool might cost you to use after a possible free trial, with $$$ to $$$ indicating the level of affordability. The tools aren't always going to be teaching and learning tools. Try them out at your own discretion; they are not recommendations on what you should be using.

New classrooms	Some of the AI technologies can be hard to imagine in a classroom or school setting. So, I try to paint a picture of a teacher in the near future, somewhere near 2030, and her interactions with new technology to accomplish her teaching goals. These aren't going to be very futuristic, that is, no flying humans, and they do not assume students have access to one-to-one computing. They also do not assume a significant shift in the teacher's instructional practices or activity choices towards more student-centered classrooms.

And a few times, I introduce a debatable complex discussion topic on AI, society, and the future. This is not grounded in factual explanation as much as it is in AI's interaction with the human ecosystem.

At the end of the book, I ground the excitement I help build up in the seven problem space chapters by sharing what I think are the biggest hurdles in our journey—but also, more optimistically, what we could do about them and why there is a case for optimism.

Why Did I Write This Book?

Actually, I almost didn't.

In late 2017, I read and heard several concerns by prominent educators talking about how AI is bad for teachers. They deemed it as something that will take away their jobs and replace teachers with robots. They argued that AI will make learning a brutally cold process. Hollywood's depictions of AI didn't help.

Having been a student of AI for a significant number of years, I thought that the reasoning behind many such arguments was shallow and uninformed. So, I thought: "why not share this alternative view of how positive AI can be?" And so, I messaged Daniel Gross, a person whose work supports new AI innovations, telling him that I was going to be writing a short article on this topic, and wondered if it was a good idea. He suggested writing a blog post article, which I agreed felt just right. But he added something that would change my plan entirely: "explain what AI really is."

Initially, That Made No Sense

I thought that the current Wikipedia article on the topic did a far better job of explaining "what AI is" than any phrasing I could come up with. **And then it hit me**. The reason why many educators were having uninformed discussions around AI was because they did not understand what AI **really was**. They treated the algorithms of AI like alchemy. They lacked an understanding of the role humans played in building AI. Moreover, they were sometimes oblivious to recent successes in machine learning but pretended to know their implications.

I couldn't blame them entirely for this. A bulk of articles and essays on AI that teachers could read and understand oversimplified a field which is filled with nuance and human judgment.

And so, I decided to do what Daniel was really asking me to do here: explain AI in the context of its potential value in education. This was never going to be straightforward, but since blogs don't get published on physical paper, I didn't worry about a lengthy blog if the content was valuable.

I kept adding details and the blog kept getting bigger and bigger. It came to the point where not many would be able to justify calling it a "blog." Calling it a book gave me room to add details that made the reading a lot less dense. And I didn't mind that!

The result of that writing process is a journey full of great details, new ideas, and optimism that I am hoping broadens your perspectives and knowledge in a direction of your interest. I am excited to have you join me on this journey!

Notes

1 "It is the science and engineering of making intelligent machines, especially intelligent computer programs. It is related to the similar task of using computers to understand human intelligence, but AI does not have to confine itself to methods that are biologically observable."—John McCarthy, one of the founding fathers of Artificial Intelligence.
2 McCarthy, J. (1998). *What is artificial intelligence?* Stanford, CA: MIT Stanford.
3 Anderson, J. R., Boyle, C. F., & Reiser, B. J. (1985). Intelligent tutoring systems. *Science*, 228(4698), 456–462.
4 See the following conferences/publications: Learning @ Scale (https://dl.acm.org/citation.cfm?id=2876034), Artificial Intelligence in Education (https://link.springer.com/book/10.1007/978-3-319-61425-0), International Society of Learning Sciences (www.isls.org/), International Conference on Intelligent Tutoring Systems (http://its2018.its-conferences.com/)

Introduction: Where We Are Today

It is an exciting time in the world of technology and innovation. Some very important chapters are being written right now in the development of computers beginning to do things only humans were able to do well so far. Leading scientists, for most of the past century, have imagined building computers that think and do what humans already know how to do well, an idea that we call **Artificial Intelligence** (AI).[1] This has, for the most part, been driven by a desire to make machines think and reason like humans,[2] whereas others have been excited by the possibility of humans forever being liberated from doing repetitive and boring tasks and instead being able to focus on the new and exciting. They imagine that this will give our species freedom, power, and knowledge like we have never imagined before.

This has barely been an overnight success story. People have been actively working on this vision since the 1950s,[3] if not earlier. But we have only recently made a round of major breakthroughs.

DOI: 10.4324/9781003183235-1

A turning point in this journey came in 2010, when, because of a "combination of big data, statistical tooling, hardware," we arrived in a "vivo state."[4] We reached a level of maturity in technology when some key historical breakthroughs in AI were ready to take flight. These breakthroughs have been a main talking point in human progress for the majority of this last decade.

But These Breakthroughs Haven't Made AI Smart Enough to Make a Dent in Many of Our Most Important Teaching and Learning Problems

The good news is that some of the very people who were working on that vision for AI in the 1950s were simultaneously or, in some cases, more seriously interested in understanding the inner workings of how the human mind learns.[5] Sometimes, working with computers to build AI was an intermediate step to uncovering the mysteries of human learning. And this led to a lot of work over the decades, which you can read a little bit about in *Appendix A: A Short History of AI for Improving Teaching and Learning*.

But in the preface, I shared my skepticism regarding the power of AI in teaching and learning today. About how we were not there yet. This apprehension in AI's value in teaching and learning today comes from its limitations. Let's discuss them.

Many of AI's advances in recent times are in **perception**[6]—the ability to see, hear, or become aware of something through the senses. But we still have a long way to go to fully realize AI's **cognitive capabilities**.[7] Computers can see, read, and capture sensory data—and recognize patterns on them rather well—but these computers don't always know what these patterns mean. Having the ability to know and understand something is called **cognition**.

Andrew Ng, one of the pioneers of this modern era of AI, has come up with a rule of thumb[8] to figure out how far AI has advanced. According to Ng, AI's potential to shine is determined by **whether a task takes less than 1 second for a human to accomplish**. If a complex task can be broken down into less than 1 second-effort pieces, it could probably be accomplished reasonably accurately by some existing AI technology. And when you think about it, you will realize that a majority of things most of us are confidently able to figure out in less than 1 second fall under the definition of *perception*.

To solidify this rule of thumb, let's look at a good example that illustrates how AI's advances in *cognition* are weak: AI, today, cannot read a textbook and go on to answer the questions at the back of the book.[9] So, current AI technology could literally be deemed to be around as sophisticated as an infant. We know that an infant's brain is known to have something called **core knowledge**.[10] *Core knowledge* allows an infant to sense and perceive the basic principles of the physical and social world like objects and sounds and touch. But it doesn't include many cognitive skills, which the infant has yet to learn. AI, today, is around there.

Fortunately, though, AI's *perception* abilities are pretty useful. An important skill in being able to perceive is to *recognize patterns*. A human's ability to tell the weather, at a given time, by just looking outside their window, and without any sensation of the air outside, is an example of **pattern recognition**. Humans have engineered computers to do these kinds of pattern recognition tasks amazingly well, but at many magnitudes faster and cheaper than it would take us humans.

And these *pattern recognition* capabilities are where AI can begin to solve some of our most painful teaching and learning problems.

Because, As It Turns Out, Teachers Perform Pattern Recognition Hundreds of Times a Day. And That Can Be Exhausting

Yes, teachers recognize patterns all throughout a class day. Sometimes thanklessly, but often endlessly.

Teachers look for patterns in students arriving and leaving the classroom on time and in an orderly manner. Teachers look for patterns in the gaze and attention of students while they lecture or pass out instructions. Teachers look for patterns when independent work is given to students, and often must make split second decisions on whether to intervene or not. Teachers look for patterns in homework and assignment submissions, to see where students consistently struggle.

All this creeps up on them very quickly, contributing to an excessive workload. This leaves them with little or no time to prioritize interventions for student success. Teachers who are unable to make every student shine everyday don't neglect individual student needs; they actually often just struggle to make sense of the magnitude of information in front of their eyes.

But over several years of teaching, teachers can become really good at these skills. In fact, in my observation, **one of the traits that repeatedly stands out in great teachers is the ability to do more pattern recognition and act on it with the least effort**.

In the evaluation instrument for Framework for Teaching (FFT),[11] also known as the Danielson Framework, one of the most widely used protocols for evaluating and developing effective teaching, author Charlotte Danielson emphasizes that effective teachers are proficient at "responding to and building upon student responses and making use of their ideas."[12]

And at a time in history when we face such a dire shortage of teachers, what education reformers are looking for very often is for young teachers entering the classroom to respond to student needs at the pace and ability of highly effective teachers. This takes time, training, and practice.

But you guessed it right. For teachers to get better at such *pattern recognition* over many years is **far from ideal**. This is neither a guaranteed natural skill one can master nor does it, in any way, solve the immediacy of the need in classrooms today. I, for one, was a horrible pattern recognizer when I was teaching in the classroom.

It is also something we don't wish for humans to be doing decades from now: repetitive tasks that take us away from what it means to be truly human. We want to spend more of our precious time **helping** students, and less of it on figuring out all the different patterns of errors made on tens of questions, while grading stacks of assessments. So, if you want to know where we can begin getting serious about AI in education, this is where you may focus your energy.

Alleviating Teacher Workload from Pattern Recognition Tasks by Using State-of-the-Art AI

We may focus our energy on using the best of what AI has to offer us today to do a lot of pattern recognition. It is that simple. In fact, let me clarify what kinds of pattern recognition tasks I am talking about here, so that we can approach these discussions with the right mindset.

We can lean on the less-than-1-second rule of thumb by Andrew Ng about today's state-of-the-art AI. Reflecting on the examples of where teachers do pattern recognition from above—the ones about teachers finding patterns in student movement, attention, independent work, and submissions—we clearly notice that in many cases, each of the micro-decisions a teacher makes to recognize a larger pattern takes him or her less than 1 second.

But what does state-of-the-art AI look like today? How might AI reduce teachers' workloads? What do these "AI techniques" look like? And what does it take for a computer to do the same thinking that human brains do so quickly?

We will try to answer these questions over the several chapters to come. But let's get started with some basics.

The Mathematical Kind vs the Non-Mathematical Kind of AI

There are a few ways to categorize the different kinds of techniques in AI. In modern AI, these different kinds sometimes blend, so some of the ways we have categorized them in the past have become inadequate. For our purposes, since we are going to focus on these techniques for most of the book, we will classify them as either the mathematical kind or the non-mathematical kind.

The mathematical kind is primarily based on "data-based AI" or AI that is numeric or algorithmic in nature. The main basis for the mathematical kind is that everything that exists in the world, including human communication and thought, can somehow be boiled down to, and captured as, some numbers (we will discuss how at a later point); this mathematics will be the basis for the AI to make decisions; and if you look close enough, you can find patterns in these numbers and you don't really need to teach the computer about how the world works. If you are a mathematics teacher, yes, I will gladly accept that telepathic high-five from you right about now!

Take, for example, some innocent sweet potatoes. If I handed you a bag of sweet potatoes, you might be able to associate numbers that represent a pattern to distinguish them from other vegetables, such as yams. You might say that, on average, a sweet potato weighs about 1.3 pounds. And on average, it is about 8 inches in length. And on average, at its thickest point, its diameter is about 5 inches. Finding the numbers to capture a pattern from many, many sweet potatoes, and then using this numerical pattern to determine whether a vegetable handed to you is a sweet potato or not, is an example of using the mathematical kind of intelligence (it is not "artificial" because you would be a human making this decision).

The non-mathematical (or more appropriately non-statistical) kind is primarily based on knowledge or logic to make machines think like humans. It doesn't disagree with the mathematical kind in the power of mathematics, nor does it entirely ignore numbers; to call it "non-mathematical" is an oversimplification (involving computers and computations involves mathematics indirectly). But instead of representing the world in patterns of numbers, it believes that for computers to understand human intelligence and decision-making, and then begin to make these decisions at a faster pace, computers can do much better by knowing the specific thinking steps involved in doing a task in the form of "heuristics" and symbols, and being able to reason with knowledge, like humans do.[13] This is similar to how we think about teaching a student to grow their knowledge and skills, except instead of a human brain, we intend to put this knowledge and skills into an inanimate computer.

To determine whether the vegetable I handed to you is a sweet potato or not, through the non-mathematical kind, you might use some simple criteria. Can you grip it in a grown-up hand? And because its diameter at the thickest point is around 5 inches, can the hands wrap all around it? If not, it might be a coconut or a cabbage, or even a carrot. If yes, is it circular or is it more cylindrical with conical edges? If it is the former, it is probably an onion or similar vegetable. If the latter, is it purplish-red in color or brown? If it is brown, you probably picked a yam. If it is purplish-red, I think I could ask a couple more questions and determine, through a non-mathematical kind of intelligence, whether you have a sweet potato or not. Don't get carried away and start cooking it just yet!

Both the mathematical and non-mathematical kind of AI are very important in their own unique ways in helping humans accomplish their goals. As it turns out, we are in the second half of an AI story being played out, in terms of the era we live in (remember what we said earlier about fast computers and too much data?), and in this half, the mathematical kind is in vogue. Over the years, the mathematical kind has been trying to borrow good ideas about knowledge from the non-mathematical kind.

While some, including me, are confident that the non-mathematical kind of AI is going to make special appearances near the climax of this story, and possibly even twist the plot, we will actually spend the first few chapters of the book focusing on the mathematical kind. That's because the mathematical kind is what has led us to the *pattern recognition* breakthroughs I have been so excited to tell you more about all this while.

Techniques From the Mathematical Kind

A lot of what we have come to know as good AI in the past two decades are many mathematical calculations involving statistics, probability, and more, wrapped into a user-friendly experience. These are calculations that computers do several magnitudes faster than humans, and calculations scientists **think** our brains are making all the time when we take in the sights, sounds, smells, feels, and tastes of the world through our senses.

But easy mathematics or hard mathematics, **what are we talking about here?**

It depends. It is a range of mathematical concepts ranging from simple to highly theoretical and complex in difficulty. On the simple end, there are concepts from middle-school algebra and high-school probability. But as one moves closer to the complex and theoretical end, the mathematics begins to get a little inaccessible to non-mathematicians. These non-mathematicians include many people who build AI technologies daily, often coming from various backgrounds and experiences.

This means that it is possible to understand the gist of it with just your memories of middle and high-school mathematics. Which means **you can understand this!**

But I am not going to make it look like it is child's play. Especially if you weren't a mathematics or engineering major in college. So, let's go slowly and steadily, and every time you want to dive deeper into a mathematical idea—put a bookmark on that page, and search online for the concepts you are getting stuck with, and I promise that you will find in-depth explanations that won't take you weeks to master. But please do not fear it, even if it doesn't make complete sense. We are not trying to be AI scientists here. We are simply trying to peek under the hood a little bit to see what the engine looks like. It is the equivalent of trying to buy a car, but instead of just being able to judge a car by its looks, we could talk about horsepower and mileage—even if we didn't understand the underlying physics.

Let's Begin By Discussing Some Basics of this Mathematics

Often, several mathematical calculations of different kinds come together to recognize patterns. And this is not just limited to AI; scientists often assume that human minds do similar calculations, often unconsciously, to recognize patterns.

Let's use a simple example to illustrate this.

> ### Anne Tries to Come Up With Criteria to Find Mistakes
>
> When a middle-school English language teacher named Anne assesses some student assignments, she keeps a running count of different kinds of mistakes students have made, in her mind. Even when students make seemingly different mistakes, like using poor sentence structures in an essay, her mind naturally tries to draw a pattern between those mistakes. She wonders: *What kinds of sentences are students unable to structure correctly?*
>
> To answer this, she may intuitively try to come up with some criteria in her mind. As a reaction to the first student's work, her initial criteria for the kinds of sentences might be:
>
> Sentences with dependent clauses
>
> *Dependent clauses* are sentences which begin with "although something, ..." or "because something, ..." (You don't need to know this to understand these terms from English language though; they are only meant for this example.)

> Now as she proceeds to grading another couple of student assignments, she begins to see some more details that help her enhance her criteria. She realizes that this may also happen when students write *compound sentences* (sentences that have conjunctions like and, but, or, for, nor, yet, so). She updates her mental criteria, while at the same time trying to use the new criteria on an upcoming student assignment to flag problems more automatically. It becomes:
>
> **Sentences with dependent clauses OR compound sentences**
>
> As she reads through a few more student responses, she realizes that it is more likely that students stumble on *compound sentences*. She now knows where her emphasis needs to be. In her mind, she has already updated her criteria to:
>
> **Sentences with compound sentences OR (to a lesser extent) dependent clauses**

It isn't uncommon for simple procedural tasks, for example grading written work, to involve creating mental criteria on the fly. In fact, in reality, in real-life examples unlike the one above, a good criterion (also called a "heuristic") quickly morphs into a complex formula of sorts. A formula that helps a teacher find a pattern in student work. And using this formula to find out the kinds of mistakes a student has made begins to look more and more like doing mental calculations. The moment we go from a simpler knowledge-driven explanation like simple criteria to something that looks more like a formula, like in the example above, we move further from the non-mathematical kind of AI to the mathematical kind.

Let's continue working on our example of Anne working with student assignments. But this time, let's actually go one step further and turn the criteria into an actual formula.

Introduction: Where We Are Today ◆ 11

> **Anne Tries to Guess How Many Students Will Pass the Assignment**
>
> Let's suppose Anne distributed a new homework assignment in yesterday's class.
>
> **And she wants to guess how well each of her students will do on the assignment, measured by what they will score**. Because in her mind, if that number is below 75, she should probably re-teach the material.
>
> She can't wait to make this guess until tomorrow because she needs to plan her lesson in advance.

Now you probably wouldn't be completely lost in trying to solve this problem had you ended up in this situation; there are a few things you know about each student and his or her capabilities. Things like:

1. the score on a similar assignment from earlier this year,
2. the score from a random assignment given to the same student last year, and
3. how attentive students were during the class period.

These clues give you some idea on how to guess a student's possible score. Why "guess?" Why not "find" or "know?"

Because if you think about it, when we act like we are recognizing a *pattern*—we are just guessing with the information we have. If I look into the notebooks of four of the students in the front row of my class and see that two of them are writing carbon dioxide as CO^2, instead of CO_2, I am going to make a guess that many more students are doing the same. I obviously don't have all the information I would ever need—of going to every student's desk and looking at what they are doing. So, I don't have 100 percent certainty until every student has turned in their work.

Having said that, let's help Anne make some guesses using what we can find.

New vocabulary

If we built some criteria here similar to the one she did in the last example, we would probably have come up with something like:

Score on similar assessment
AND (to a lesser extent) last year assignment score
AND (to an even lesser extent) student attentiveness

Intuitively, this is a rough place where we could begin. We know that there are always a few students who are ahead of others in the class. And to avoid listening to the material they already understand over and over again, they stop paying attention and do something else instead. So, student attentiveness is not the most representative of how they will perform. So, we lower the importance of student attentiveness.

Even then, this is some very rough criteria, and it doesn't help us accurately pinpoint whether or not each student might score over 75. A mathematical way to approach this, which might give us the number we are looking for, would begin with coming up with a **variable** for each kind of clue. Say,

1. "a" for *score on similar assignment*,
2. "b" for *last year assignment score*, and
3. "c" for *student attentiveness*.

Using these *variables*, we can turn the criteria into a formula:

`Final score` = a + b + c

This is a good start, but this lost the emphasis on certain criteria over others. We may bring back some emphasis on some *variables* over others, by multiplying each of the *variables* with something. We don't know those somethings yet. Nevertheless, when we multiply a *variable* with a number, that number is called a **coefficient**. And adding *coefficients* into our formula, we come up with:

`Final score` = (coefficient 1 * a) +
                (coefficient 2 * b) +
                (coefficient 3 * c)

> Now you may remember from middle-school algebra that such a formula or equation that had *variables* in it was called a **function**. You may remember using the *function* `f(x) = mx + b` for representing a straight line on a graphing paper. In that *function*'s case, *m* is a *coefficient*. (If you don't remember that *function*, I am guessing you were a playful one!) And the b in the function `f(x)` is different from the *variable* b we created above for *last year's assignment score*.
>
> Using the *function* notation, we finally end up with:
>
> ```
> f(a, b, c) = (coefficient 1 * a) +
>              (coefficient 2 * b) +
>              (coefficient 3 * c)
> ```

Having a rough formula based on some criteria is a great start. But how good is such a *function* if one can't plug in *a*, *b*, and *c* values to get a guess of how much a student will score? Remember, we don't know what the *coefficients* are yet!

As it turns out, we can try to find out these *coefficients* by using some historical data and a little mathematics. A few students in an advanced mathematics course in your area's high school might be able to do this. They might call this a **line of best fit** or **linear regression** problem.

However, when these students try to find what these *coefficients* should be, they will need some help from us. They will need us to tell them for several homework assessments in the past that had **different combinations of *a*, *b*, and *c*, what score did Anne finally see for each student**. Were individual students' assignment performances mostly based by how they performed on the previous test? Or was attentiveness in the classroom the most important factor? The more of such data we can give them, the better *coefficients* they will come up with.

New vocabulary

We have some of this data on hand. Let's go through an example where we only take into account *a*, or *score on similar assignment*, and try to see what those advanced mathematics students may have done.

The data looks something like this (say scores are out of 100):

TABLE 1.1 Scores of six students on two different assignments: a new assignment that they recently took, and a prior similar assignment

Student no.	Score on new assignment	Score on similar assignment
1	28	32
2	43	41
3	90	99
4	71	85
5	96	84
6	66	43

Yes, it would be ideally nicer if we had more data to come up with a *function*, but to keep things simple, let's limit the number of examples to six students.

One of the things you may remember from middle-school algebra about simple *functions* with a single *variable* is that they can often be plotted on a graph. So, let's try to see if we can put these points on a graph in trying to come up with our *function*. When we put a point with two numbers on a graph, we arbitrarily assign one of its numbers to represent the horizontal axis **x**, and the other to represent the vertical axis **y**. Let's try to do the same here.

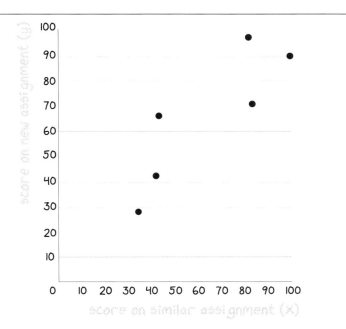

FIGURE 1.1 Scores from new assignment and similar assignment plotted to show relationship

The premise of a statistical idea called *linear regression*, the one we said those advanced mathematics students would have used, is that there is a line that runs through the graph and least deviates from the points on it. And the equation for this line is indeed the best *function* for guessing the unknown. In our case, that unknown would be the *score on new assignment*.

Why might the line that least deviates from these existing points help us guess the position of a point not already on it, though? That's because we think that there is a pattern here, specifically a "linear" one, which is the same as saying that the pattern might be a line. And if we are given an x value, and no y *value*, our best bet would be to say something along the line of: looking at how other x values were related with their y values, we can place the points on an imaginary line that runs in the direction closest to all other points.

Here, the mathematics of *linear regression* would involve using the averages of both kinds of scores, and the distance between the line created by the averages, to find the *coefficient* to x (and a little remainder in the form of another number) of the best fitting line, which would give us:

$$f(x) = 0.81x + 13.8$$

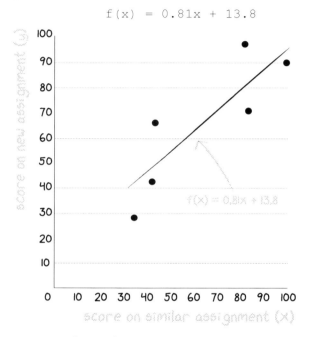

FIGURE 1.2 Scores from new assignment and similar assignment, with function that best fits the line, using regression

This means that if we plug in the scores on similar assignments of all students as x in this equation one at a time, we can guess their likely individual score on our new assignment.

And eventually, we can take an average of all the guessed scores. If the average turns out to be over 75, Anne can probably get away without re-teaching the material.

Don't worry if this mathematics seems confusing; only re-read this section or find external sources if you can't get a broad understanding of what is happening here.

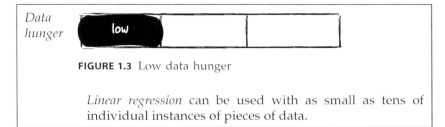

FIGURE 1.3 Low data hunger

Linear regression can be used with as small as tens of individual instances of pieces of data.

More data would have made the *coefficients* we found above even better, making our *function* an even better score guesser. This idea around more data makes sense intuitively too. Experienced teachers are consistently better than novice teachers at making these guesses because they have seen so many more students. So, in the end, their mind has more data points.

New vocabulary	**Data** is an extremely important idea to understand in the mathematical kind of AI, and modern AI in general. You probably feel like you somewhat understand it. But talking about it in very simple ways will help us refresh the most basic notions in your mind.
	Let's consider our example above. The numbers that capture student performance in the past are a form of data. They could have even been alphabetical grades. In this case, we had it in the form of a neat table. Most often, they come in tables or in another structured way. But many other times, they come unorganized. Have you ever seen sequenced human genetic data? Or perhaps accidentally opened a file with a text editor when it is not meant to be opened there? This seemingly unorganized data, mixed with symbols, numbers, alphabets, waves of signals, etc. is all data. Sometimes we know how these are organized and represented, but sometimes we don't. For example, if we put all the symbols on an ancient Greek cave wall into a computer, even though it is data, we might not know what these symbols represent and whether they are structured in the form of sentences or some other system.

What about things in the world that don't look like data? Is the air in the room you are in also some kind of data? Or the leaves on trees outside your house? You are right, they are not data. But humans have invented sensors that turn the physical world into data. Air has a vast number of physical properties; like speed, temperature, color, composition, smell, etc., each of which can be measured by some sensor. The same case is true for leaves.

Data doesn't have to mean that it is on a computer, even though that is the most common use of collecting data. That's because computers can analyze data way faster than humans. It could be on a piece of paper or a notebook, or just be constantly flashing on a screen in front of you on an LED panel, like at the banks and government offices. Or it could be knowledge in your mind about how to teach a unit on prepositions or adjectives, that you could explain to a new teacher. But as you might have learned during the most basic study of statistics or probability, more data (as opposed to little data) is always better to build a clearer understanding of what is going on.

Now, people are generally talking about lots of the same data in a collection, when they use words like **dataset**, **corpus**, and **examples**. It often means lots of data that looks alike. A *dataset* doesn't mix student performance data and teacher retention data; it is homogeneous in some way.

When thinking about why we need data at all, it is important to remember a simple principle, which is as true in discussions that don't involve using any technology: **if something can't be measured or captured as data, it can't be analyzed or understood well, leave alone improved**. In education, data has been around for more than a century—in the form of students producing work and the grades they get. Every other progressive discipline of study is extremely reliant on data. Being against data is equivalent to being against progress and reasoning. It is like being an engineer designing a bridge and not being interested in measuring the dimensions of the pieces that form the bridge, nor using those measurements in the final bridge design process. We know that London bridge is going to come falling down, my fair lady!

Introduction: Where We Are Today ◆ 19

The example we worked through to guess scores on new assignments had only a little data and one simple *function*. We mentioned earlier that, in reality, formulae, or *functions* as we call them now, can be very complicated. And to make them good, we need a whole lot of data. Coming up with these *functions*, and then evaluating a new student's work on it to make guesses of final scores or see other *patterns*, can take a teacher non-trivial amounts of time.

New vocabulary	In mathematics, such a *function*, which after being setup with *coefficients* reflects a *pattern*, is called a **model**. And *variables* like x that were needed from before are called **inputs**. The final result of the *function*, the guess, is called an **output**.
	Coming up with this *function*, the *model*, is probably the most important step in coming up with a phone or computer application that can be used by a teacher to *recognize patterns* in the classroom. Unsurprisingly, it isn't easy to come up with one that is based on a lot of data and works in a variety of situations. Actually, for any task that is even slightly complex for humans, you can be assured that coming up with this *function* is hard, and the *function* is likely hard to understand itself—with too many squiggly lines and symbols. But since coming up with this *function* is our goal for each new task, scientists keep tweaking their attempts until one recognizes the intended *pattern* well.

Using our new terminology, we could say that in an example where Anne is trying to guess scores on the new assignment, the score on a similar assignment, last year's assignment score, and student attentiveness were the *inputs*. And our final determination on how likely the sentence is going to be structured incorrectly is the *output*.

And so, one wonders, why can't we make a computer come up with the *model* by taking in information coming from students' work or the classroom? After all, we know that the computer would do this faster because it can do many more magnitudes of calculations than our brains can at one time. And if we can program the teacher's computer with this *model*, it could make these guesses all day long for us.

New vocabulary	**Machine Learning (ML)**—a term you have probably heard a lot recently—revolves around doing mathematics that helps us come up with these *models*, so that we can get solutions when we try to guess something.
	The big idea in *machine learning* is to create the best possible *coefficients* to a *model*'s *functions*, which gives us the most accurate guess for a given set of *inputs*. Since this is done by a computer and not those students we had volunteered earlier, it has the word "machine" in its name. This is done by a computer without being programmed to do so.[14]
	So, we make guesses or approximations or inferences, or as we will call it from now on, we make **predictions**. And that is exactly our goal in m*achine learning*: to make better *predictions*. If our current *prediction* is correct 7/10 times today, let us try to make it correct 8/10 times by tomorrow.
	As a result, scientists often try to spend their energy trying to optimize these *models* by "**maximizing**" their quality of *predicting*—another way of saying that they are constantly tweaking it until it *predicts* the *pattern* well. Until it is as close to perfect as possible. Just like Anne did in the first example of grading essays as she saw one student's response after another, until she had something she was happy with. By *maximizing*, I don't mean always try to show the most positive result. That would be **biased**. I mean a *model* whose *output* reflects the most accurate, most realistic result.
	Sometimes this involves *linear regression*, similar to what we saw in our example from above. And other times, it involves other mathematics, some of which we will cover in upcoming chapters. But more often than not, each problem where we try to make a different *prediction* requires coming up with a different *function* with such optimal *coefficients*. There is no one *function* that solves all problems.

So, circling back, all we are really trying to do is to make a great *function*. Why? Because once we feed information from what is happening in the class and in student work into this *function*—it will *predict* what is going on. And if all of this is done by a computer (or AI, whatever you want to call it), we just saved a teacher precious brain time and effort. The teacher can now use this newfound time to focus on planning his or her next moves instead.

New vocabulary	But in trying to come up with the *function*, we might realize that just one simple *function* with linear terms (e.g., just x without any power, unlike x^2 or x^3 or so on) might not be enough to make a good *model*.
	In those cases, we might realize the need for polynomial terms. Polynomial terms might, for example, make x more important by making it to the power of 3 or 4 or 5 or more, like x^8.

By the way, these *functions* or algorithms can get fairly complex and actually hold tens or even hundreds of *variables*, with *coefficients* on most of them. It makes them much more versatile, as the complexity increases. Which is going to happen in 3, 2, 1…

Because what if this puzzle can't easily be solved by one complex *function*? Maybe it needs one complex function after another? It turns out that as *prediction* problems become increasingly complex, it becomes very difficult for a computer to figure just one *function* to make perfect. Like in our example, at some point the line might not give us very accurate results with such few and simple *variables*.

It reminds me of those long-response questions in mathematics assessments in high school where the answer could only be derived after taking the solution of one equation and feeding it into another, and so on.

And That's Where Deep Learning Came In

A few smart mathematicians[15] essentially had the same idea. But in the 80s and 90s, they didn't have computers fast enough to come up with such complex *functions*.

Remember how we said that in 2010 everything changed? To put it simply, this is exactly what had changed by then. Computers became fast and cheap enough to stack these *functions* one on top of another to come up with very complex *functions* that now worked with software that could run these calculations well. And there was an abundance of data to *maximize* them.

New vocabulary	The process of *maximizing* these stacked *functions* is called **Deep Learning**, consequently becoming an important sub-field within *machine learning*, and thereby important to AI in general.
	These stacked *functions* often residing in "**layers**"—each a little individually simpler than before because we are not trying to directly come up with just one perfect *function*—are called **neural networks**. These attempt to mimic the process of one kind of guess of how the neural networks of the human brain work.
	In these, each *function* uses the answers of some previous ones to get the next solution. So, in theory, while you could merge them all into one very long and complex *function*, splitting them into individual simpler *functions* allows the people coming up with these *networks* to do a lot of advanced mathematical manipulations easily. It is the same principle we use to teach elementary school students to dissect, decode, and infer letters and phonemes in a word, words in a sentence, and sentences in a paragraph.

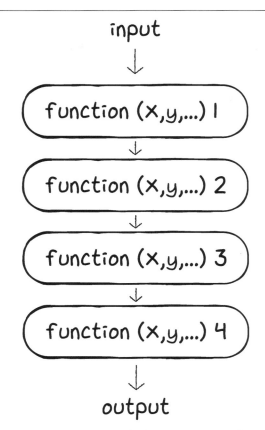

FIGURE 1.4 A simplified representation of a neural network

Like the case of *linear regression*, scientists provide the data to the computer to come up with each of the stacked *functions*. Through trial-and-error, they also try and suggest which *functions* would be most appropriate, such that when their *coefficients* are *maximized*, the *prediction* is closest to what they expect it to be.

Now the computer can much more accurately determine the perfect *coefficients* to all *variables* in each *function*. Voila!

| Data hunger | 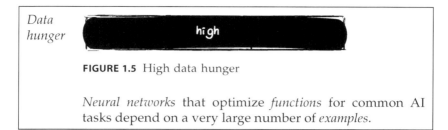 |

FIGURE 1.5 High data hunger

Neural networks that optimize *functions* for common AI tasks depend on a very large number of *examples*.

Using this elementary and very incomplete understanding of the state of AI, we can now begin to discuss some recent big ideas in this field, in the context of problems we ought to solve to reduce teacher workload.

But before that, I must admit that it does feel like I am saying that to solve some of our problems; like the examples on essay grading and assignment score *prediction*, AI needs to depend on mathematical *models*, which are optimal formulae. Mathematical *models* are only one part of the whole story.

| New vocabulary | *Machine learning* is one of the more popular sub-fields in AI. It is the mathematical kind. It is not the same as AI; AI is a bigger set of things. |

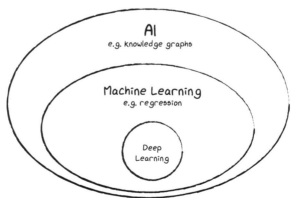

FIGURE 1.6 A diagram showing how AI is bigger than machine learning, which is also a large superset of things

AI contains sub-fields that may or may not be the mathematical kind themselves, but may be complemented by mathematical techniques, like the techniques of *machine learning*.

I promise we will discover more AI than just *machine learning*, but because *machine learning* is such an important reason for why we are discussing this in the first place, I thought it would be a good idea to get it out of the way.

I bet you didn't think that I'd give away most of the secret sauce (i.e., *deep learning* and *maximizing a model's functions*) in the very first chapter. This makes me a non-ideal person to talk to about a new movie that I just saw; I would probably give away the spoiler too soon!

Notes

1 Russell, S., & Norvig, P. (2020). *Artificial intelligence: A modern approach* (4th edn). Boston, MA: Pearson.
2 *Professor John McCarthy—Contributions and impact* (n.d.). Retrieved October 1, 2019 from: http://jmc.stanford.edu/contributions/index.html.
3 Dartmouth workshop (2019). In Wikipedia. Retrieved from https://en.wikipedia.org/w/index.php?title=Dartmouth_workshop&oldid=1018409510.
4 Fei-Fei Li et al. (n.d.). *Past, present and future of AI/machine learning (Google I/O '17)*. Retrieved May 19, 2017 from: www.youtube.com/watch?v=0ueamFGdOpA.
5 Doroudi, S. (2019). *The intertwined histories of Artificial Intelligence and education (Draft)*.
6 Ng, A. (2016). What artificial intelligence can and can't do right now. *Harvard Business Review*, November 9. Retrieved from: https://hbr.org/2016/11/what-artificial-intelligence-can-and-cant-do-right-now.
7 Newell, A. (1994). *Unified theories of cognition*. Cambridge, MA: Harvard University Press.
8 Ng (2016).
9 Tenenbaum, J. (n.d.). *MIT AGI: Building machines that see, learn, and think like people*. Retrieved February 8, 2018 from: www.youtube.com/watch?v=7ROelYvo8f0.

10 Spelke, E. S., & Kinzler, K. D. (2007). Core knowledge. *Developmental Science*, 10(1), 89–96.
11 Danielson, C. (2013). *The Framework for Teaching Evaluation Instrument, 2013 Edition: The newest rubric enhancing the links to the Common Core State Standards, with clarity of language for ease of use and scoring* (2nd edn). Published by Charlotte Danielson.
12 Danielson (2013).
13 Brock, D. C. (2018). Learning from artificial intelligence's previous awakenings: The history of expert systems. *AI Magazine*, 39(3), 3–15.
14 Samuel, A. L. (1959). Some studies in machine learning using the game of checkers. *IBM Journal of Research and Development*, 3(3), 210–229.
15 LeCun, Y., Bengio, Y., & Hinton, G. (2015). Deep learning. *Nature*, 521(7553), 436–444.

2

Feedback and Scoring

It should come as no surprise to anyone that teachers spend an enormous amount of time grading/assessing student work and giving them feedback to do better. This is often extremely repetitive and mundane work.

It's probably also the first thing that came to your mind when we talked about pattern recognition and making *predictions*. And that's because this is happening not just during class time when the teacher is checking for student understanding across a packed classroom and trying to change her plans on-the-move. It's actually eating up teachers' personal lives. Spouses and children are no strangers to the stacks of student work brought home and graded in the evenings during what should be a teacher's National Geographic binge-watching time. Pssh … I am kidding—nobody that exhausted ever watches National Geographic in the evenings!

This massive time suck is something that should bother us all.

But There Are Much Larger Problems With Such Manual and Painful Ways to Assess Learning That Should Worry Us

Around the world, in examinations and as a direct consequence, in teaching towards success in examinations, **the questions asked of students often are very "shallow."** If you aren't familiar with the word "shallow" to describe a question, it usually means questions that require you to regurgitate facts after you have done some rote memorization.[1] They often begin with "what" and "who," and don't require any analytical thinking. They are also called "lower-order" questions.

Unfortunately, examinations and standardized tests (the most common form of "summative assessments"), where these questions are dominant, drive curriculum and consequently instruction in a significant majority of classrooms around the world.[2] So, you end up with textbook-driven learning, and what students learn in class is trying to jot and memorize the answers to more of the lower-order questions than to contemplate reasoning to ones that put emphasis on analysis and creativity—which we could call "higher-order" or "deeper" questions. There is no room for open-ended group discussions, project-based learning, and critical thinking with the former kind. Even though such learning inadequacies are directly rooted in the systems around assessment, it is the teachers who get blamed for low levels of student engagement in classrooms. **This is unfair**.

Moreover, people who study education and society will often draw a connection between a disengaged and unready workforce AND an entrenchment of lower-order thinking in education systems.[3] The link is undeniable.

But do you know why, after decades of research and reform pushing for shift to more "higher-order" learning, education systems are struggling to move away from lower-order thinking and learning?

Because it is **very hard for humans to grade higher-order questions.** It is very hard for administrators to train hundreds of thousands of teachers to grade such questions in any cost-effective and consistent ways. Especially as, year after year, nuances in the questions change, teachers need to regroup and recalibrate themselves on how to assess these questions.

You already know this. It takes much less human effort to assign a score (say, out of 5) to a student response to the question:

1. list the events that led to the Crimean war.
than it does to:
2. what alternative strategic choices would you have made as a leader in the Russian army to increase your likelihood of success?

But if AI's *prediction*-making can alleviate parts of the process where a human assigns the score and constructs feedback, you can begin to imagine a shift in your examination questions towards higher-order questions. And that will lead to practice questions in the classroom moving towards higher-order thinking. And you know where I am going with this; eventually, we are talking about everyday teaching and entire education systems moving away from rote memorization. *The dream.*

So, Solving This Problem, in Many Respects, Is the Key to the Holy Grail

That said, it's important to realize this is hard to do. In fact, it's so hard that there is a phrase for this kind of a problem; such a problem is called an **AI Complete**[4] problem. An *AI Complete* problem is one whose solution, when found, will solve all the most pertinent problems of AI, making AI as cognitively capable as humans. This is because assessing higher-order thinking involves accurately understanding and assessing human knowledge, actions, and opinions reflected in a student's own words. Which is arguably among the highest levels of human capabilities.

So, let's not get ahead of ourselves here, especially after we already established that AI's cognition skills are weak today. Unlike humans, computers today have their own mechanism for perceiving the world before they begin to understand what's in that world.

New vocabulary	When we humans see a table of information, say a menu in a restaurant, it doesn't matter how this information is presented to our eyes to capture it, because our eyes and minds develop the ability to perceive and organize the contents of the table rather quickly, regardless of whether this information were presented on a handwritten blackboard behind the counter, printed out on a menu card, flashing on a 50-inch TV screen, or browse-able in a tablet app. On the other hand, for computers, these are all very different things, and they do better on perceiving some things over others.
	For computers to perceive information, at the very minimum, the information must be something that can be stored as numbers. It can't just be a physical thing in the world. Because at the end of the day, computers are simply giant calculators that are proficient at storing and processing numbers.
	For example, computers have been very good at perceiving and working with language, ever since their early days. We all remember opening up some form of text editor and creating documents when we used a computer for the very first time. This invention exists, in part, because there is a universally accepted system for language that can be mapped to numbers. You could say, "a" is 1, "b" is 2, "c" is 3, and keep going until you have assigned a number to each symbol in each language in the world. When you saved a document, it saved your deepest thoughts as a series of numbers that computers could store and retrieve.
	Now, what is not universally easy to explain and map is how these symbols are used in the language we speak, and that is where AI will play a role. We will talk about this soon.

> What about physical things in the world that are not numbers? We earlier discussed how data can be captured by sensors. The most common way of taking something in the physical world and trying to make computers perceive it is to take pictures and put them on a computer. In these cases, cameras become their eyes. And microphones become their ears. While there is no one-to-one mapping to other sensory organs, different sensors may capture touch, smell, and taste. Computers also perceive the physical world when we interact with keyboards and mice and 3D sensors. Anything from these sensors can be turned into numbers.

But before we continue to ask how AI can reason about student responses (the cognition bit), allowing us to pose and assess more higher-order questions more often, we need to answer a more basic question: how might AI perceive student handwriting in notebooks, worksheets, and tests, and talk in classroom discussions or performance? Things that aren't just computerized numbers.

It starts with our friend from the last chapter: *deep learning*.

New vocabulary	A perfect example of computers trying to understand human work is them trying to read our handwriting or older printouts when we scan something, and turning them into words and sentences so that we can paste them in MS Word. That's exactly what we want computers to do for a scanned set of unit assessment response sheets, for example.
	This is called **Optical Character Recognition** (OCR).[5] Remember that software on your computer, the one that came free with the scanner, that produced unconvincing results even on printed documents? That's OCR.
	You could do OCR with or without *machine learning*. However, in recent times, scientists discovered that they could produce much more convincing results on images of handwriting using deep learning.[6,7]

> *Tool to try* — Dropbox ($$$), the application on your computer that magically syncs your files across computers, uses modern *machine learning*—primarily *deep learning* techniques we will discuss soon, to understand words and sentences in scanned documents and pictures. This allows organizations using the tool to store tens of thousands of documents to quickly search for specific words written in these documents.

Oh, hang on, one second. How did *deep learning* go from a set of complex stacked *functions* (or a *neural network*, as we called it) with *coefficients*, to reading handwriting and spitting out words? What kind of a *prediction* is that?

If you think about it for a minute, you might be able to convince yourself that it is a *neural network* that takes in some numeric *inputs* of handwriting, say one letter at a time, and gives us a *prediction* of how likely the letter is "a" or "b" or "c" and so on. But how did we turn handwriting into numbers?

> *New vocabulary* — You probably already know that each little dot in a digital picture is called a **pixel**. That's why you have a 2 megapixel (2048 pixels) camera, or a 5 megapixel camera, or a 10 megapixel camera, etc. When we scan a piece of student work, we are taking a digital picture of the work. This scan is basically a digital puzzle full of square dots—a file that has information on thousands of pixels of the page. Since it's a written response paper that we are scanning, you can assume we scanned it in black and white.
>
> Do you know what information each black and white pixel conveys? It simply conveys a number between 0 and 100 on how black the pixel is, with 0 = white, and 100 = pitch black. Let's zoom in on a sample handwritten alphabet to see how these pixels might be conveyed.

Feedback and Scoring ◆ 33

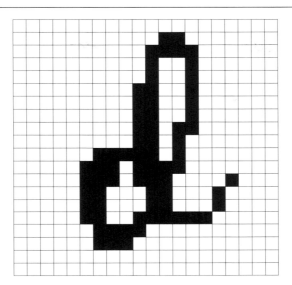

FIGURE 2.1 A zoomed-in scan of a handwritten letter, as a composition of pixels

FIGURE 2.2 A zoomed-in scan of a handwritten letter, represented as a mathematical matrix of levels of black and white

> To you and me, this could be an "a," "l," or a "d." But a computer sees each of the smaller boxes as a number between 0 and 100.
>
> So now, suddenly, we can see each piece of student work as lots of rows and columns on a grid of pixels. Do you remember from high school how we placed lots of numbers in rows and columns into something that we can perform mathematical calculations on? In **matrices**, of course! The infamous *matrices*—which had no evident practical value when we learned them—but now, suddenly, they are very useful.
>
> Using this same way, we can turn pretty much any image—writings and drawings included—into a *matrix* of numbers.

So far, whenever we saw a mathematics *function*, we assumed it only worked with whole numbers, like 3, 5, 10, fractions like 1/4 or 8/5, or numbers with decimals, like 21.04, 0.93, etc. But as you may remember from when you learned this in high school, *matrices* can also be placed in an equation and multiplied, divided, added, and subtracted with. Therefore, using *matrices*, most things that are not a number in plain sight can be turned into one. And consequently, these *matrices* become the *inputs* to our *neural networks*, and we can make *predictions* with them!

Anyways, back to scientists making progress and using *deep learning* (and here's where the mathematics begins to become slightly complex, and so I avoid diving too deep into it).

New vocabulary

Coming up with a sequence of stacked *functions* which make a *neural network* good is some bit art, and a whole lot of experimentation. But that is the essence of making *deep learning* solve new problems well; trying new and innovative "architectures" of *neural networks* until the *predictions* become very good.

But what do I mean by "architectures" of *neural networks*? Earlier, when I showed you a visualization of a *neural network*, I kept things simple. One *function* on one line, and one line on top of another. In reality, modern *neural networks* often have many *functions* on a single line, or on a single *layer* as it is often called, with the *output* of one *layer* often, but not always, directly flowing to the next *layer*. For illustration purposes, consider these drawings:

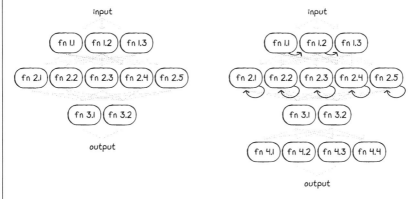

FIGURE 2.3 A couple of simplified neural network architectures. "fn" is short for function

One of the early highly consequential breakthroughs for *deep learning* that gave excellent *predictions* was an architecture of stacking *functions* called **Convolutional Neural Networks (CNNs)**. *CNNs* worked remarkably well for making predictions that recognized the contents of images.[8] Put very simply, the word *convolutional* implies that there are convolutions in the neural network. And *convolutions* are a fancy way of saying *functions* that summarize or distill the results of multiple other *functions*.

> If we consider the example of recognizing handwritten letters, we know that in trying to identify an entire letter—which might seem like a trivial skill to your brain today—a computer must first be able to identify points, and then straight lines, and curves, before *predicting* the entire letter. *Convolutions* do just this; its lower-level *functions* solve sub-problems and then summarize the results to higher-level *functions* stacked ahead of them in the *neural network*.
>
> This idea extends to recognizing objects, faces, and entire scenes in images. Images are nothing but compositions of smaller visual elements stacked in complexity to create a whole. Thus, *CNNs* work well for solving image-recognition problems, among others.

Just like many other successes in *deep learning*, we can't always easily scientifically show why, but using *convolutions* in a *neural network* to *predict* the right handwritten letters worked like a charm! It even did very well against illegible handwriting (yes, I am looking at you, my doctor, Dr. Thomson!).

Scientists tested the **accuracy** of such *models* by providing scans of letters written by hundreds of other people, plugging them in as *matrix inputs*, and looking at the final *predictions* to see how close they were to what a human would have perceived them to be. One of the main ways scientists use to test how well designed the *model* is in solving the problem is by testing how good the *predictions* of the *model* are on never-seen-before data.

And eventually, stitching these letters together, they could decipher whole words and sentences.

New vocabulary	But what if the *model* picked up some letters incorrectly because a few students wrote them in, to be polite, very unique ways?
	Say, for example, that a sentence written by a smart 2nd grader is read by the *model* to be:
	T-h-e · p-e-n-c-i-l · i-s · b-e-d

Feedback and Scoring ◆ 37

> This makes no logical sense, really. I don't know anyone who would sleep on a bed of pencils, really. Also, the student was asked to describe objects, not write imaginatively. We wish the computer read the whole sentence and could find misrecognized letters.
>
> We can use something called a **language model**[9]—for now, a big *function* that *predicts* the best words that follow a word in a sentence—in combination with computerized versions of the Webster or Oxford Dictionary. Together, they can identify a better possible series of words, and consequently, be able to correct the spellings of wrongly recognized handwriting. Alternatively, the same techniques can flag spelling and grammar errors. All this happens through *predictions* made using *machine learning*.

Data hunger

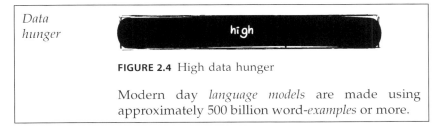

FIGURE 2.4 High data hunger

Modern day *language models* are made using approximately 500 billion word-*examples* or more.

So, they found a way to make this whole handwriting recognition technology even better by using a dictionary. Who knew that digital versions of those fat books catching dust in our corner shelves would be so useful, even today!

And so, sticking to our theme of *screen-less* classrooms, that's how *deep learning* is helping to perceive handwriting in the case that students aren't typing their answers into a computer. But in case you already have one-computer-per-child in your classroom, this first step isn't necessary.

> *Tool to try* — Gradescope ($$$) is a grading assistant tool that helps you grade faster once you scan in student work into the app. Gradescope takes all student assignment work and uses *Convolutional Neural Networks* to *predict* which pieces of student work look identical to each other. Such that once you have graded and left feedback on one kind of student work that likely repeats in the responses of other students, you do not have to do the work of grading and providing feedback against a rubric all over again.

But students are producing evidence of their learning in one other big way.

Specifically, What State-of-the-Art AI Exists to Help Us With Student Talk in Class Responding to a Teacher's Questions?

What about AI understanding this kind of, what is often called, formative assessment?

After all, what they say during the class in-between activities and in discussions is a very important source of information on a student's level of fluency with the material and with his or her ability to articulate responses well in spoken language. Tied with written work, we can begin to capture an evolving picture of what the student is producing around the content they learn.

> *New vocabulary* — Let's back up a little bit.
>
> Before we entered this new "vivo" state of AI in this past decade, and seriously until only a few years ago, we were also not very good at using a microphone to turn speech into text. Such a computerized conversion of speech to digital text is called **Automatic Speech Recognition (ASR)**.[10]
>
> But you probably know what happened next: *deep learning* changed this too. Just like AI, I am becoming rather "predict"-able here. Ba dum tss!

> Using another interesting type of *neural network*—this time **Recurrent Neural Networks (RNNs)**[11]—the accuracy of sound going into a *model*, and spitting out correctly recognized spoken phrases as text, skyrocketed. Just like we converted images to a numeric form, in this case, audio chunks were converted into *matrices*. The rule of thumb remains: if it can be digitized, and shared over email or on USB sticks, it can probably be made into numeric values like *matrices*.
>
> What are *RNNs* and what mathematical trick did they really do?
>
> Sometimes, *inputs* are in the form of sequences of things that all depend on each other to create meaning in the world. Think about a dance. Each movement is often meaningless and might look like an odd body movement. But when sequenced one after the other, in a certain order and cadence, it creates beautiful meaning which we can all appreciate. Mostly. I still don't get break dance.
>
> *RNNs* are good at *prediction*-making based on such sequences. Mathematically, to accomplish this in a set of stacked *functions* of a *neural network*, a solution from one *function* is used to recognize a few previous *inputs* into a *function* to *predict* a set of new *inputs*.[12]
>
> This idea works very well in recognizing speech in audio, which can be understood as a sequence of sounds which only make sense as a whole and not as separate audio chunks.

Woah—that was confusing! When we earlier discussed *neural networks*, it mostly looked like only one new set of *inputs* were going in for each time we needed to make a *prediction* on some data. And using these new *inputs*, the set of stacked *functions* passed their result from one to the next, eventually producing an *output*. This resembled an assembly line of workers in a car factory, all doing their portion of work, which they passed along the line to the next worker. Sometimes two or more workers did work together at the same step before passing it forward.

But *RNNs* seem to make it look like the workers along the assembly line are doing something else. It seems like they are holding onto some extra pieces and scraps used in the previous cars as they work on the new car assembly. Going back to mathematics, how and why are we able to do this in coming up with a *neural network model*?

The explanation is a little hairy here—so if you want to dive deep, I recommend studying *deep learning* separately. Understanding the mathematics is not crucial for you to continue enjoying reading the book, so it's completely okay to turn a blind eye to this if it is too dense. But mathematics teachers: you should have no excuse here—this stuff is your bread and butter.

New vocabulary	Let's go back to what we discussed earlier. In *machine learning*, we are always trying to figure out the best *coefficients* to a complicated *function*. And in our previous example, we did this by doing some mathematics—specifically *regression*—to find the *coefficients* using lots of examples of data.
	In *deep learning*, this big idea continues; except there are many stacked *functions* whose *coefficients* we need to figure out. The most common way we do this, called **backpropagation**,[13] is a little bit more complex. So, let's read it as steps:
	1. We pass the *inputs* of our examples (where we already know the final *output*, or answer key, for each example), one-by-one through our stacked *functions*, our *neural network*.
	2. But hang on, the *coefficients* haven't been set so far! So, initially, we just set some random numbers on them so we can get an *output* to that *function* and pass it to the next one.
	3. As it goes through all the *functions* and *outputs* come out through the last *function*, we compare the *output* from the *network* to what our answer key, the original *output* from the example, was. We knew the answer key all along, of course. So, for example, we may have been looking for the number 5 in our answer key to some specific *inputs*. But we might get 8.

> 4. Then we use an idea from high-school **calculus**, that you probably remember called **differentiation**, to find out better *coefficient* values. Here is a brief explanation if you are curious:
>
> This difference from the comparison of the output to the answer key in the previous step, called the **error**, is the feedback we need to know. It tells us how good or bad the *coefficients* are. If we were looking for 5, and we got 8, the error is 8 − 5 = 3.
>
> Using the *error*, we go back and adjust the *coefficients* slightly, trying to make it such that the next time around, the *error* will be lower. This adjusting of *coefficients* using the *error* involves using, if you are interested in the mathematics, the "chain rule."
>
> Now, we repeat these steps with the same or more examples and answer keys over and over again, until those *coefficients* become very good—thereby giving us a good *model*.
>
> This whole process of putting examples through the *neural network* to *maximize* the *coefficients* is called **training**.

The more diverse the examples you give to the *network*, the more able it becomes at *predicting* diverse *inputs*. A *neural network* that has seen a large number of examples has adjusted its *coefficients*, and therefore the underlying mathematical formulae, more times to the point that the *prediction* seems better at *inputs* it hasn't seen before. These *networks* are just like humans in that way; as we grow up and see and do more of something, or gain more experience, we get better and faster at it as compared to a novice.

So, if we take speech from lots of students with diverse accents, and do *training* on them, we have a much better shot of the AI identifying what that student from South Africa is saying.

Talking about South African accents, one of the complexities of picking up what students are saying in their native ways of expressing themselves is trying to figure out the context of their words and actions. What they just said is significantly influenced by the words they uttered before that. Because if you think about it, every few words we utter only make sense when we know the words uttered before it—when we have context. This changes from language-to-language and culture-to-culture. Some part of our inability to perceive students' needs stems from our limited mental ability to keep track of so much context for so many students.

Even in our first languages, when we accidentally mishear or tune out in lengthy monologue-heavy conversations (sometimes colloquially referred to as "rants") and don't remember what our spouses said in the previous sentence, what do they tell us?

"You Are Not Paying Attention To Me"

Can we improve *Automatic Speech Recognition* by allowing *Recurrent Neural Networks* to pay proper attention to context in sequences?

New vocabulary	We already know that *RNNs* focus on the idea that during *training*, instead of just treating the new *inputs* as a completely fresh set of *inputs* to the *neural network*, we preserve and use a little information—the solutions of some of the *functions* in the middle—from the previous few *inputs* in the sequence.
	The idea that helps *RNNs* pay adequate, but not excessively distracting amounts, of attention to *inputs* in a sequence is, unsurprisingly, called **attention**.[14]
	Attention is a concept that explains how much emphasis—in the form of bigger or smaller *coefficients* on variables in a *function*—the *network* should place on the last word before the current word, the second-to-last word, the third-to-last word, and so on. A well-*trained* network with the optimal value for these *coefficients* drastically improves the *predictions* made in *RNN models* involving sequences.

Tool to try	Before *deep learning* became good at turning speech into digitized text, organizations hired human transcriptionists to type out the words they heard in audio recordings of the conversation. Descript ($$$) is an app that uses *RNNs* to turn an uploaded audio or video file into a high-quality transcription and gives you an easy editing tool to fix mistakes or remove unnecessary bits.

All that's well and good, but classrooms are chaotic and students aren't walking up to perfectly placed microphone stands and pushing their lips into the microphones while speaking. What about when sound is coming from a distance in the room? How useful will these *RNNs* be then?

New vocabulary	Major microphone hardware improvements, tied with *deep learning*, have also made breakthroughs recently in **far-field voice recognition**.[15] Voice is *far-field* when the device listening to the sound is not near the human speaker, so the sound *input* into the *model* is very faint. Additionally, such *input* has background noise and "reverberation." Reverberation is when sound hangs around in the air even after it has been created because it reflects off different surfaces.
	Prediction in these cases can only be good if a *model* was *trained* on *far-field* examples. In the absence of good *far-field training* examples, a technique used by some scientists has involved adding fake noise and reverberation on clean (or sometimes called **red**) *near-field* (normal close-to-microphone) audio *training* data.
	Specialized hardware, often with several microphones on it, has had an important role to play in the process. These several microphones are placed in what are called **linear arrays**—formations of placements on the device. Picking up multiple "channels" of sound from different places on the device means that the *models* can learn the *coefficients* of things like noise and reverberations, thereby improving their *prediction accuracy*.

> *Tool to try* In 2014, Amazon launched a home device called Echo ($$$) with a personal assistant called "Alexa" that people could speak to. While this wasn't the first voice-enabled personal assistant, it was one of the first commercially viable *far-field voice recognition* devices. This was possible due to specialized hardware built in close connection to the voice recognition system and a lot of *training inputs* on voice that came from across a room.
>
> Since then, Google has also built a popular *far-field* voice assistant device called "Home" ($$$), while Apple's voice assistant Siri can be found in a device called HomePod ($$$$).

So, if you can capture what students are saying through one or more microphones and take good looking photos of their written work, you can now digitize them. Digitizing them is a prerequisite before AI can perceive them using techniques like *CNNs* and *RNNs*.

And Perception Is a Prerequisite Before AI Can Analyze Them

Aha—now, we get to the heart of things! And that heart is taking text—transcripts of words said and typed-out written work and assessing the quality in response to an expected level of performance.

We obviously are hoping to go further than bubble sheets (like the ones used for grading a shaded option among A B C D or E), merely catching simple spelling mistakes (like in MS Word), and auto-grading simple response types or only programming assignments. These things are useful, but don't change our ability to assess answers to higher-order questions.

That is why advancements in the field of **Natural Language Processing** (NLP)[16] are going to be enormously important. They are going to be important in understanding questions, in understanding answers, and in understanding everything expressed in written form around the world.

So, let's get our feet a little wet here.

New vocabulary	*NLP* is an AI field containing several sub-fields made of many techniques,[17] some more mathematical than others. It's a big, complex, yet very interesting field. All these techniques primarily focus on using text—in our case the written and spoken responses of students—to *predict* something about their grammar/syntactical structure (for demo example, see https://cloud.google.com/natural-language/), and consequently its semantics and meaning. This is sometimes referred to as **text analysis**.

Tool to try	Quill ($$$) is a tool that uses *NLP*'s building blocks to identify poor writing quality—a critical aspect of student-produced work across subjects. Quill claims to *predict* poor sentence fragments in student writing 40 percent better than Microsoft Word or Google Docs and immediately provides feedback to the student. Grammarly ($$$) is a browser extension that does something similar, but with a focus on simplifying professional written communication. ETS's e-rater ($$$) has a similar goal and came long before modern *NLP* techniques.

Data hunger	medium **FIGURE 2.5** Medium data hunger *Text analysis* techniques may or may not depend on the use of *machine learning*. When they do not involve *machine learning*, they do not need a huge *dataset*. Instead, they often benefit from rules of syntax and grammar that emerge from commonly found text in a particular language.

In some cases, a few simple techniques are very useful. When we are looking for one-word responses, we just want to *predict* if the student said "chlorophyll" when I ask them about the green pigment in plants. Even if this is written as a sentence, basic understanding of the sentence's syntax allows me to find this answer by reading, for example, the subject and object of the sentence.

Knowing the syntactic structure is a prerequisite to identifying grammatical errors, like poor sentence structures and the start and end of phrases, once we have already taken care of identifying misspellings thanks to *language models*. And knowing the meaning of each sentence and how those sentences come together is a prerequisite to evaluating their quality.

But again, we are interested in assessing the deeper meaning of the response, for the computer to understand the idea and not just a few words here and there.

New vocabulary	The sub-field primarily focused on going beyond syntax is called **Natural Language Understanding (NLU)**.[18] Its goal is for computers to really understand the gist, the connected details, the connections, and purpose of some piece of text.
	As a result, *NLU* is wide in its scope, so let's start slow. We will learn more about *NLU* in the chapters to come.
	One of the basic building blocks of *Natural Language Understanding* is called **syntax parsing**. It is the process of dissecting a sentence into "parts-of-speech" like a Grade 5 English teacher would do. The process in which you discover the subject, the object, and the verb of a sentence, apart from other things.
	One application of syntax parsing is in a sub-technique called **intent parsing**. Intent parsing allows a computer to take a request like "wake me up at 7am" and chunk its words and phrases, consequently turning the word "wake" to a new alarm in its alarm app for "07:00" on the forthcoming day. And sure, you can hit snooze after that all you want.
	This required a little more than understanding the syntax—the computer had to have known that "waking" is tied with the idea of alarms. And this waking action is often associated with a time.

But student work is a little more complex. It is disorganized thoughts, it is text and drawings, it is formulae, it is showing the student's process on the side and crossing off wrong answers, it is filled with shrills of excitement and murmurs of embarrassment and more.

And thus, here's the more humbling place where we are today. Even with the existing wonders of *NLU* research, evaluating the quality of open-ended student work is not a well-solved problem. There is more work to be done.[19] And that means there is more work before we solve the holy grail: assessing responses to higher-order questions.

This dismay is not limited to just assessing student work; such complexity of written human expression is also at the heart of our inability to, for example, flag fake news.

> *Tool to try* Although AI cannot assess open-ended student work in its entirety, *NLU* advancements are used in a tool called Duolingo English Test ($$$). It is an English language proficiency certification that assesses both native and non-native students' reading, writing, speaking, and listening skills. This makes it possible to assess student language skills at a much smaller cost than traditional English proficiency examinations graded by expert humans.
>
> Pearson's Versant ($$$) and IntelliMetric ($$$) are other tools to accomplish similar results, while tools like TurnItIn Revision Assistant ($$$) and Project Essay Grade ($$$) focus specifically on essay grading and feedback, making it a kind of **Automatic Essay Scoring** tool.

I realize that you probably wished I had a happier ending. So here are some optimistic ideas of what we can do with our existing *NLU* strengths—ideas that weren't possible only a few years ago—that I want to leave you with:

- Use pre-written rubrics[20] to evaluate the quality of student open responses, short and sometimes even long.[21]
- Capture, automatically group, and prioritize the most common misconceptions—using pre-unit surveys.

- "Listen in" to every group discussion simultaneously and assess patterns of student talk and equal engagement.[22]
- Conduct a simple assessment of proficiency of student reading ability by analyzing their read-alouds and identifying vocabulary interventions. Similarly, conduct a shallow assessment of student written work for prioritizing areas of language practice. These are both extremely vital for getting a deeper sense of English Learners' (ELs) areas of struggle.[23]
- Use more custom matching of texts with a student's current reading abilities (rather than forced bucketing into reading levels) such that they form a progression to the grade-leveled readers.

New classrooms	Meet Ms. Nelisa Wuku. And imagine that she teaches English language and social studies to a classroom of 32 students at a public school in a medium-sized town in your country. She has three to four hours of classroom instruction scheduled every day.
	She likes to give students "exit tickets"; these are written slips at the end of the class period for students to showcase their understanding. It used to take her about an hour to review these tickets for every hour of classroom time. Now, after the class period, when she walks into the staff room/teacher's lounge, there is a machine next to the photocopier that resembles a bill counting machine at a bank. She first puts in a single exit ticket; this one has been written by her and has the expected correct answers for non-open-ended questions. The machine gives her a green sign asking her to feed student responses.

She puts the stack of the 32 exit tickets into the feeder, and it rushes to process all sheets in 45 seconds. The machine scans the tickets, figures out the sentences students have written, and dissects the phrases and words to understand their meaning. It then compares the student responses with the answer key that Ms. Wuku put in earlier. This machine is connected to the printer, which promptly begins to print two pages of report on these exit tickets. The report shows her what percentage of students performed poorly, groupings of right and wrong student responses with examples, and names of students who need attention. If there was a question about student wellness and comfort on the ticket, it summarizes the results and lists the outliers.

In the past, Ms. Wuku used to struggle to keep students on task, equitably engaged, and producing good work during small group work. Sitting in on one group's discussion means that she could not help other groups at the same time, and that group's students generally felt pressured.

Nowadays, things look better. She places a small wireless hand-sized home speaker-like microphone device on each group table anywhere the group chooses to have their discussion.

And she sits in her desk on one side of the room with a tablet or laptop computer, where she can switch between tabs on different student groups on an app. Each tab shows the transcript of the conversation between the students that only she can see. She can also see how long each student spoke and some statistics around choice of topics discussed. This allows her to track the progress of each group and drop in and offer suggestions in the right direction, or praise for good work done so far. This also allows her to effectively evaluate individual contributions, no matter the output of the group. It also allows her to consider an alternative student grouping that is more effective for the future.

Notes

1. Mehta, J., & Fine, S. (2015). *The why, what, where, and how of deeper learning in American Secondary Schools* (Students at the Center: Deeper Learning Research Series). Jobs for the Future. Retrieved from www.jff.org/resources/why-what-where-and-how-deeper-learning-american-secondary-schools/.
2. And that's also why you responded to more "shade-the-right-circle" kind of questions on national or international exams like the SAT, rather than writing or typing your detailed views in paragraphs.
3. Wagner, T. (2008). Rigor redefined. *Educational Leadership*, 66(2), 20–24.
4. Mallery, John C. (1988). *Thinking about foreign policy: Finding an appropriate role for artificially intelligent computers.* The 1988 Annual Meeting of the International Studies Association, St. Louis, MO.
5. Optical Character Recognition (2021). In *Wikipedia*. Retrieved from https://en.wikipedia.org/w/index.php?title=Optical_character_recognition&oldid=1016528333.
6. Cireşan, D. C., Meier, U., Gambardella, L. M., & Schmidhuber, J. (2010). Deep, big, simple neural nets for handwritten digit recognition. *Neural Computation*, 22(12), 3207–3220. Retrieved from https://doi.org/10.1162/NECO_a_00052.
7. Michael, N. (2015). *Neural Networks and Deep Learning*. Determination Press. Retrieved from http://neuralnetworksanddeeplearning.com/chap1.html.
8. LeCun, Y., Bottou, L., Bengio, Y., & Haffner, P. (1998). Gradient-based learning applied to document recognition. *Proceedings of the IEEE*, 86(11), 2278–2324. Retrieved from https://doi.org/10.1109/5.726791.
9. Language model. (2021). In *Wikipedia*. Retrieved from https://en.wikipedia.org/w/index.php?title=Language_model&oldid=1023428386.
10. Robust automatic speech recognition. (2016). *Elsevier*. Retrieved from https://doi.org/10.1016/C2014-0-02251-4.
11. Graves, A., Mohamed, A., & Hinton, G. (2013). Speech recognition with deep recurrent neural networks. *Proceedings of the 2013 IEEE*

International Conference on Acoustics, Speech and Signal Processing (pp. 6645–6649). Retrieved from https://doi.org/10.1109/ICASSP.2013.6638947.

12 RNNs explained well here: https://distill.pub/2016/augmented-rnns/.

13 Werbos, P. J. (1990). Backpropagation through time: What it does and how to do it. *Proceedings of the IEEE*, 78(10), 1550–1560. Retrieved from https://doi.org/10.1109/5.58337.

14 Vaswani, A., Shazeer, N., Parmar, N., Uszkoreit, J., Jones, L., Gomez, A. N., ... & Polosukhin, I. (2017, December). Attention is all you need. In *Proceedings of the 31st International Conference on Neural Information Processing Systems* (pp. 6000–6010).

15 Lu, J. (2017, August 5). Can you hear me now? Far-field voice. *Medium*. Retrieved from https://towardsdatascience.com/can-you-hear-me-now-far-field-voice-475298ae1fd3.

16 Natural language processing (2021). In *Wikipedia*. Retrieved from https://en.wikipedia.org/w/index.php?title=Natural_language_processing&oldid=1024275775.

17 Read more here: https://en.wikipedia.org/wiki/Natural-language_processing#Major_evaluations_and_tasks.

18 Allen, J. (1988). *Natural language understanding*. San Francisco, CA: Benjamin-Cummings Publishing Co., Inc.

19 McShane, M. (2017). Natural language understanding (NLU, not NLP) in cognitive systems. *AI Magazine*, 38(4), 43–56.

20 Rubrics can be written as long-wound sentences on multiple dimensions of student responses, which takes a teacher some thinking on where the student response lies OR, as it turns out, and as research has shown, teachers use rubrics much more effectively when the rubrics can be broken down into small and simple yes/no questions for presence of certain elements from student responses. This idea reminds us why AI can succeed at this approach— based on Ng's framework, they are <1 sec decision tasks. That said, increasingly, advancements in *NLP* are allowing us to capture and represent more complexity in sentences, making the case for AI that can evaluate student work based on richer, more detailed rubric statements as instructional designers prefer.

21 Michalenko, J. J., Lan, A. S., & Baraniuk, R. G. (2017). Data-mining textual responses to uncover misconception patterns. *Proceedings of the Fourth (2017) ACM Conference on Learning @ Scale* (pp. 245–248). Retrieved from https://doi.org/10.1145/3051457.3053996.
22 Segal, A., Hindi, S., Prusak, N., Swidan, O., Livni, A., Palatnic, A., Schwarz, B., & Gal, Y. (Kobi). (2017). Keeping the teacher in the loop: Technologies for monitoring group learning in real-time. In E. André, R. Baker, X. Hu, M. Ma, T. Rodrigo, & B. du Boulay (Eds.), *Artificial Intelligence in education*. New York: Springer International Publishing, 64–76. Retrieved from https://doi.org/10.1007/978-3-319-61425-0_6.
23 I have seen my mother struggle with students' challenges here all throughout her teaching career. It is really unintuitive to do this at scale.

3

Improving College Readiness

Upon reading the title of this chapter, you may have wondered how making students readier for college and possibly a career is related to the theme of this book of improving how AI can support teachers teach in their day-to-day tasks of supporting student learning. It isn't, directly. But indirectly, every *pattern* a teacher tries to recognize has some bearing on the future success of a student. And we know that teachers don't teach just because it is how they can make a living. They often get invested in the long-term success and growth of their students and, consequently, entire communities. So, each action, and each recognized *pattern* is critical to a student's learning journey.

And if talking about examinations and standardized tests allowed us to understand why teachers weren't going "deeper" into the material, talking about college and careers can help us understand some of the purposes of examinations and standardized tests in the first place.

But more selfishly for both you and me, it allows us to study important ideas in AI further here. It also is a little bit of a breather from so many new difficult concepts we have discussed in the previous chapter.

So Let's Dive In

Let's begin with a place where we, as humans caring about other humans, have traditionally struggled with solving the college readiness problem. Students from low-income households have disproportionately been much less likely to go to and graduate from college.[1] This lowers their expected quality of life and earning ability,[2] leaving them with the label of being "at-risk" students[3]; that's if we pay enough attention to them in their K–12 school. **"At risk" of not being successful**.

And when we do identify them to be "at risk" while in K–12, we also know that if it's early enough, we can take the right steps within their time inside and outside the classroom to re-engage them and provide support.[4]

Humans may be slower than machines, but sometimes we don't need a lot of numbers to tell us the story—we know who is least likely to do well on the SATs or the standardized examinations, or if he or she is going to take the test at all. We have enough big and clear signals of the risk.

But what happens when we fail to identify that risk early? Normally, when we know something or someone is "at risk," we panic! We call the ambulance or the cops or a psychiatrist. But we have all had times in life when it has been just a little too late. Sometimes seconds, sometimes months, and sometimes years. And our excuse for not knowing earlier has always been: "but I couldn't tell!"

Do you know why you couldn't tell?

Patterns are interesting things. Sometimes, they don't seem pronounced enough when they start, even though the brain is constantly trying to make such predictions.[5] Especially because, based on what we know, the brain can only reasonably attend to one thing at a time.[6] My rough hypothesis is that our brain's most active pattern recognition portions—the hippocampus and the ventromedial prefrontal cortex[7]—are constantly, in their own neurological way, tussling with each other, saying "hey I have a better pattern" or "hey check my big pattern out—you got nothing!" Each of these pattern recognition tasks are competing for your time, your energy, and often your dopamine.

But I think we can all agree that anything that helps us see patterns and helps us change lives sooner rather than later is extremely valuable. Fortunately, AI does not struggle with recognizing a lot of different kinds of patterns at the same time. It also doesn't compare them with others for your attention.

New vocabulary	Let's go back to *machine learning*, where we strive for the best *pattern recognition*. And let's pick up a little bit of terminology along the way.
	In our assignment score predictor from Chapter 1, a *linear regression* example, we were expecting the solution to the *function* to be the expected score of individual students.
	In the example on *predicting* letters, however, I changed things up without giving you any warning. Since a single score wouldn't have told us much—we needed to *predict* how likely a small part of scanned handwriting was an "a" or "b" or "c" or so on. We needed to predict a number denoting the likelihood or probability that a letter *input* belongs to this **class**, with "a," "b," "c," etc. being different *classes*.
	This gives us the technique of **classification**. As you may have guessed by the name, *classification* is aimed at *predicting* the degree to which an *input* belongs to a *class* or group. *Classification* belongs to a small spin on *linear regression* called **logistic regression**.

Data hunger	low		

FIGURE 3.1 Low data hunger

> Just like *linear regression*, a simple *logistic regression model* can be made with as little as tens of individual instances of pieces of data. However, as your expectations for your *model* to make good *predictions* on many scenarios grow, the *training* data your *model* needs, for it to do a good job, also grows.

Classification problems are very common too. In our classrooms, when we differentiate instruction, we are constantly classifying kids by ability levels.[8] When we line them up, we are classifying them by heights and gender. When we are making heterogeneous reading groups, so that proficient readers can help weaker students, again, we are classifying students. This is very much an extension to what we earlier discussed about *pattern recognition*. We also do bad *classification* sometimes—when we let our *bias* classify students poorly, without even realizing.

Most importantly, however, focusing on our need of the hour, having any kind of data on students over a longer period helps us classify some into being "at risk."

To help us get there, let's continue working on our made-up example of Anne working with student assignments. This time around, let's try to figure out how the mathematics behind *classification* might work, by building on our homework assignment scenario.

> **Anne Tries to Guess Which Student's Assignment She Is Looking At**
>
> We left off at the point where Anne had given her students the assignments and tried to make a *prediction* on individual student scores, the night before.
>
> Say her students came to class the next day and turned in their assignments. For one of the assignments that got turned in, a student forgot to write his or her name on the top. **Can Anne identify the student just by looking at the responses?**

> She is home now, the grades need to be turned in before midnight, and there is no chance she will be able to ask the class about this one tonight.
>
> Now, in real life, she wouldn't need the mathematical fanciness we are about to explore. She could just go through a roster of students and place a check mark against the names she has seen so far, and then end up with the student who doesn't have a check mark against his or her name. But for the sake of learning new things, let's pretend like that simpler option didn't exist.

Again, we know that we can count on a few clues that will help us distinguish between different students' works. These include a student's:

1. Handwriting,
2. Writing style,
3. Similarity to his her/previous work.

New vocabulary	Let's continue with our mathematical practice of giving a *variable* for each kind of clue. Say,
	1. "x" for *handwriting*,
	2. "y" for *writing style*, and
	3. "z" for *similarity to previous work*.
	We (or the computer) can come up with a mathematical *function* using individual *variables* representing each clue. But this *function* couldn't possibly tell us the name of the student who forgot to write their name at the top. It would merely give us a numeric value as an *output*, right? How would that value represent a distinct student that we are trying to identify?
	Suppose the classroom has a student named Jonathan. And let's identify him by his roll number "1."

Turns out that if your *function* is good enough (in this case, holds all the distinct *variables* that represent the uniqueness of student writing), your *function* will be able to return an *output* from 0 to 1 (or 0 percent to 100 percent likelihood) that indicates how likely the assignment is Jonathan's. For this, we will provide Jonathan's roll number as one of the *inputs* to the *function*. The *function* will be able to return this likelihood because the *function* would have been *trained* on examples. When these are examples of Jonathan's work, they have a distinct *output* value uniquely representing his *class*.

An *output* of, for example, 0.82 or 82 percent, will tell us the level of certainty that this is Jonathan's assignment. We can do the same with the rest of the students by assigning each student with distinct *class* values (we can continue using their roll numbers) and determining the likelihood that it is a particular student, from the *output*.

Yes, that does, for now, require us to shape the *function* to produce several *outputs* for each assignment, one *output* for every possible *class*. This is called **one-vs-all**. These *classes* could look like:

...
2: Julia
3: Kamaal
4: Laura
5: Rowan
...

Eventually, when we have everyone's *outputs*, we can compare them to find the highest percent *prediction*. That's the student Anne is looking for.

Tool to try	Teachable Machine ($$$) is an experiment by Google Creative Lab that helps you quickly and easily create a *classification model* using webcam *input* and actions you take with hand and face gestures that you give *classes* to. For example, the tool can use your webcam to take pictures of you making three facial gestures—smiling, frowning, and confused—a few times each. And then, when it says the *model* is ready, it can *predict* the *class*, in this case the facial gesture, that your expressions intended.

Often, there are data points in our school databases, particularly in "Student Information Systems," that have the necessary historical assessment performance information needed to *classify* students, with one possible *class* being "at-risk" students. The big advantage with computers doing *classification* on the data we already have is that they can do this number-crunching the whole time in the background without any human explicitly working on it.

But to do that, the data and *functions* would need to be prepared from before. There's probably some part of you wondering which one of your overworked colleagues would sit and make these amazing *functions* and label x, y, and z on student records. And even if they are going to do all that work, whether that data even has the answers to classify the "at-risk" students.

But let me challenge our plan to use *classification*, in the first place.

I believe that in a sizable number of schools where students are found to be "at risk," several eyeballs go through the final scores on student assessments. The class teacher, the parents, the vice principals, possibly classmates, etc. If these student performance records were all that we needed to find who was at risk, we would have done that a long time ago without fancy technologies. The report card would have been the best AI in the world.

But no, they often fail to do the job.

Because Many Times, When Trying to Understand Complex Human Patterns, There Is no Well-Described Data

We have signals—lots of noisy *perception* signals from what we see, what we hear, and how we feel. But we have no explanation of the data of these signals. We fail to see patterns entirely, even after trying with all our heart.

Imagine having a bunch of *x*, *y*, and *z* data, but no idea which students they identified, in the examples to perform *regression*. That would have made it nearly impossible to create *models*. Or would it?

New vocabulary	*Machine Learning* techniques can be categorized into two types: **supervised learning** and **unsupervised learning**.
	Supervised learning is what we have been talking about thus far.[9] When we have known everything about the data that we wanted to analyze to build a *model*. We discussed an example to *predict* performance on a new homework, where we had a bunch of data points from before where *a*, *b*, and *c* (representing *score on similar assignments, last year's assignment score*, and *student responsiveness*, respectively) have been associated with the final homework assignment score. In the example just above, we have also had some examples matching *x*, *y*, and *z* to specific identified students, as well as the **output** for each example.
	Unsupervised learning is when the data isn't matched to an *output*. In a way, this is when we don't have a concrete meaning assigned to it already. For those kinds of problems, there are other techniques. And one such famous technique is **clustering**.
	Clustering is a technique that identifies groups (or "*clusters*") of individual data records which seem similar to each other. Unlike *classification*, where humans can also easily find patterns—*unsupervised learning* can be used to find patterns in data that humans often don't know exist.
	But the mathematics in *clustering* works slightly differently from *regression*. Instead of trying to find one perfect *function* that gives us a number, we just want to find what cluster each *input* belongs to, such that *inputs* in the same clusters are closer to one another than *inputs* in different clusters. And so, our goal in *clustering* becomes figuring out what these *clusters* are and where you draw the lines around one vs another without having well-*labeled* data.

Tool to try	Google has created *unsupervised learning models* ($$$) that can *predict* lung cancer from CT scans well before a trained radiologist is able to.

If you are fond of the *Harry Potter* story like I am, imagine that we are in the first few years of Hogwarts opening and no houses exist yet. The headmaster is disappointed in the lack of student competition at the school and invents the "sorting hat" to create student houses of students that feel similar to each other (remember how it almost put Harry into Slytherin?). But it doesn't have any prior record of which house students belong to or how similar they are to one another. So, unfortunately, no easy criteria to form the houses. And so, for the very first year that it is introduced, it goes around Hogwarts, identifies likely similar people, and makes an arbitrary criterion to group students. This grouping results in four houses, although it could've been any number. Over the years and seeing more students, it improves because it has house assignments for prior students. If *Harry Potter* were real, the sorting hat would be an excellent practical example of an *unsupervised learning model*, specifically a *clustering model*.

These non-easily classifiable and non-easily data-organizable problems are more common than you would first think. An example is when we can't even plan to understand why certain groups of students will drop interest from science and mathematics.[10] This happens despite us capturing all the data in the world but being unable to fit the pieces together. That's when systems designed to tell us a story through *clustering* can help us.

So, whether it is *linear regression* or *logistic regression*, or even *unsupervised learning* techniques like *clustering*, we now have an insight that allows us to act. But do we always possess the skills to act on their challenges?

Moreover, Can AI Help These Students?

This is a large and open question, but we can begin to try and envision possibilities using some simple grounded reasoning and experimentation by going through at least one example.

We earlier talked about the students who are disproportionately more likely to be "at risk." One such example is students from families where English (or whatever the primary language of instruction is) is not the first language spoken at home. Because if a student can't follow his or her teacher's instructions or easily connect with their classmates, isolation and low engagement with the content makes him or her more likely to be distracted and lose interest in the process of learning.[11]

I can never forget feeling completely powerless when my 4th-grade Latino student gave me completely blank stares after I narrated the steps to the science experiment we were all going to do. I could tell that, while he had heard most of the words I said, my sentences made no sense to him. I was losing him drop-by-drop with every lesson.

I later wondered: why should patterns only be recognized by teachers? Why can't we enhance students' pattern recognition skills by using AI? Without removing the teacher from the picture.

We earlier talked about AI understanding student speech. Students whose first language isn't the primary language of instruction (say, English) could surely use all the help available in understanding teacher speech. But how would just speech turned into text help them? Especially those who are as unfamiliar with the written language as much as the spoken one, if not more.

It would make a world of difference if AI helped them perceive the patterns in their language.

New vocabulary

NLP has another sub-field of interest to us: **Machine Translation**. Which means computers taking text in one language and translating it into another.

Just like some of the other things we talked about, prior to using *deep learning*, scientists were not as successful as they would have liked to be. Using *deep learning*, *Machine Translation* has seen some massive success, using approaches that may be called **Neural Machine Translation** (NMT)[12]—because of, you know, our good friends: *neural networks*.

The innovation was, again, in the architecture of the *neural network*. We continue to use *attention*, but we add a new concept called **sequence-to-sequence** (specifically the **encoder–decoder** type), which is also used in *Recurrent Neural Networks (RNNs)*. Remember from the introduction on *RNNs* that the *network* uses previous *inputs* to make a *prediction* on the current *input*? This is particularly useful in the context of translation and language in general because words change meaning based on the words that precede them. So, a good *prediction* of a word's meaning may be based on words before it or the context it is used in.

The big idea in *sequence-to-sequence* is that sequences of words in the source language—in our example from above, English, are converted into *matrices*, something we have discussed earlier. The process that converts them to *matrices* are what we call the *encoder*. The *matrices* are then fed into a series of *functions* in our *neural network*. And then only after the last *function*, words are plugged back from the destination language—in our example, Spanish—replacing those *matrices* (the *decoder* piece). So, it tries to *predict* a mapping of a sequence of words in one language to another. This is attempted to be visualized in Figure 3.2.[13]

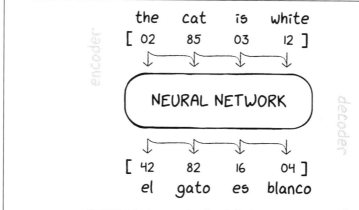

FIGURE 3.2 An overly simplified representation of a sequence-to-sequence neural network for machine translation (inspired from PyTorch's visualization of NMT)

This, tied with *language models*, our means to *predict* correctness of words and sentences, allows us to make higher quality *predictions* of translations.[14]

Tool to try	Microsoft Translator ($$$) is a chat app where you have textual conversations with people who can type in different languages, but the messages are instantly translated and presented to a user in their primary language. Using the same idea, an app called TalkingPoints ($$$) allows teachers, who natively speak English, to have chat conversations with parents, who aren't comfortable English language speakers, through SMS chat.

Now, *Machine Translation* would be very useful if that student didn't have to wait to get a printed and translated transcript of my instruction several minutes after I uttered some information.

I could think about how cool it would be if, while I spoke in English (because I could not possibly afford to lose other students with my broken Spanish), a live professional translator spoke my words in Spanish into a headphone my student wore.

Improving College Readiness ◆ 65

Like they do at the United Nations. Or **simultaneous interpretation**, as it is called. I would look so much like Leonardo Di Caprio giving a global warming address every single day. Oh, I am such a hopeless dreamer. Or am I?

Maybe there is no need for a human to do the heavy lifting here as well.

New vocabulary	We talked about *Automatic Speech Recognition* as something that converts speech into text. And *Machine Translation* that converts text from one language to another.
	What if we could make *neural networks* that combined the two worlds: by taking in speech (as *matrices*) and giving us translations into another language? Much like the simultaneous interpreters at live events do. Turns out, some scientists did make such *neural networks*, and they call this form of simultaneous interpretation **Simultaneous Machine Translation**.[15]
	This is mathematically more complicated to explain because the order of words in a sentence spoken in one language does not match those in another. But because everything must happen simultaneously, the *predictions* need to be made not just on what had just been said, but on what has yet to be said based on what has been said in the source language.
	Here is an example[16] of how the *prediction* looks when the *Simultaneous Machine Translation* succeeds:

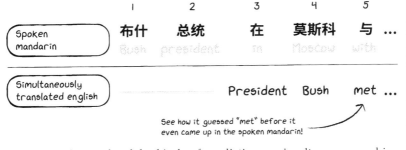

FIGURE 3.3 A sample of the kinds of predictions a simultaneous machine translation has to make (adapted from STACL by Ma et al.[17])

It isn't entirely clear how this might play out in a classroom; either a screen in the front of the classroom showing the live translations in multiple languages, or a specialized piece of transparent eyewear for students with the text read out in the corner of their eyes. Or perhaps taking the technology further, the translated text could be read out in some way, using technical breakthroughs we will talk about soon, into a non-intrusive headset.

Tool to try	Google's Pixel Buds ($$$) and Baidu's WiFi Translator both allow you to listen in on an audio conversation in another language and have it instantly translated and played out to you in your primary language.

Whatever the actual product may look like, we can imagine it being the norm in classrooms with such students by the end of the next decade. I know this sounds futuristic. But just imagine how futuristic handheld computers seemed in the early 90s and see where we are today.

Now, this is just one example of how a challenge some "at-risk" students face can be drastically reduced because AI can help bring capabilities in the classroom that the teacher just couldn't do with her limited time and linguistic abilities.

This Is Just One of Many Possible Interventions to Reduce the Disproportionate Readiness for College and Career

But it is a huge step in the right direction. It enables us to reduce injustices that have kept the playing field uneven, as for decades we demanded that English Learners (ELs) forcefully and unnaturally catch up on English before they enter the classroom. This was not only unfair, but it was also often infeasible.

Inclusive learning environments require that we treat ELs as individuals who bring "assets" to the classroom, instead of liabilities.[18] *Machine Translation*, for example, allows us to engage ELs by:

- Using words from their language in our conversations with them, to engage them and trigger their prior knowledge as they remember it in their own words.
- Allowing them to use words from their own language in responding to us verbally and in the written form until they pick up the English counterparts. Only when they feel truly intrinsically motivated and heard can they focus on the content and gain a richer exposure to English.

Whether it is identifying "at-risk" students or enabling them to recognize the patterns that a world different from theirs imposes on them, AI can enable several magnitudes more time and attention spent on their needs.

New classrooms	In most classrooms in the world, English is not the language of instruction. This might be true with Ms. Wuku's classroom too. But unfortunately, a lot of interesting supplementary learning material on the Internet and in encyclopedias is locked in English.
	Ms. Wuku now begins by searching for good geography resources on the Internet, in English. In the past, when she found just the right report or article that she wanted to have her students read in class the next day, she painstakingly began translating it into her primary language of instruction herself. This process took hours.
	Instead, she now opens a website where academic text can be automatically translated into a language of her choice. She copies the original article and pastes it on this site. This site gives her a translated version in her non-major language in seconds.

Notes

1 Choy, S. P. (2002). Access & persistence: Findings from 10 years of longitudinal research on students. Informed Practice: Syntheses of Higher Education Research for Campus Leaders.

2 Christle, C. A., Jolivette, K., & Nelson, C. M. (2007). School characteristics related to high school dropout rates. *Remedial and Special Education*, 28(6), 325–339. Retrieved from https://doi.org/10.1177/07419325070280060201.
3 Dix, N., Lail, A., Birnbaum, M., & Paris, J. (2020). Exploring the "at-risk" student label through the perspectives of higher education professionals. *The Qualitative Report*, 25(11), COV4+. Retrieved from https://link.gale.com/apps/doc/A643343967/AONE?u=sacr16736&sid=AONE&xid=3f67b949.
4 Perna, L. W., & Swail, W. S. (2001). Pre-college outreach and early intervention. *Thought & Action*, 17(1), 99.
5 Sacrificing accuracy to see the big picture: *Our ability to detect patterns might stem, in part, from brain's desire to represent things in simplest way possible.* (n.d.). *ScienceDaily*. Retrieved March 5, 2018, from www.sciencedaily.com/releases/2019/03/190305153641.htm.
6 Miller, T., Chen, S., Lee, W. W., & Sussman, E. S. (2015). Effects of processing multiple auditory feature patterns: Multitasking. *Psychophysiology*, 52(9), 1140–1148. Retrieved from https://doi.org/10.1111/psyp.12446.
7 This is your brain detecting patterns: *It is different from other kinds of learning, study shows.* (n.d.). *ScienceDaily*. Retrieved May 31, 2018 from www.sciencedaily.com/releases/2018/05/180531114642.htm.
8 Tomlinson, C. A., Brighton, C., Hertberg, H., Callahan, C. M., Moon, T. R., Brimijoin, K., Conover, L. A., & Reynolds, T. (2003). Differentiating instruction in response to student readiness, interest, and learning profile in academically diverse classrooms: A review of literature. *Journal for the Education of the Gifted*, 27(2–3), 119–145.
9 LeCun, Y., Bengio, Y., & Hinton, G. (2015). Deep learning. *Nature*, 521(7553), 436–444.
10 Raabe, I. J., Boda, Z., & Stadtfeld, C. (2019). The social pipeline: How friend influence and peer exposure widen the STEM gender gap. *Sociology of Education*, 92(2), 105–123.
11 Takanishi, R., Le Menestrel, S., National Academies of Sciences, Engineering, and Medicine (U.S.), National Research Council (U.S.), National Research Council (U.S.), National Research Council (U.S.), National Research Council (U.S.), & National Academies of

Sciences, Engineering, and Medicine (U.S.) (Eds.) (2017). *Promoting the educational success of children and youth learning English: Promising futures*. Washington, DC: The National Academies Press.

12 Bahdanau, D., Cho, K., & Bengio, Y. (2014). Neural machine translation by jointly learning to align and translate. *arXiv preprint arXiv:1409.0473*.

13 Robertson, S. (2019). *NLP from scratch: Translation with a sequence to sequence network and attention—PyTorch tutorials documentation*. Retrieved from https://pytorch.org/tutorials/intermediate/seq2seq_translation_tutorial.html.

14 If you want to dive into the mathematics, I recommend going through the external tutorial: Neubig, G. (2017, March 10). *Neural machine translation and sequence-to-sequence models: A tutorial*. Retrieved June 29, 2019 from the arXiv database.

15 Gu, J., Neubig, G., Cho, K., & Li, V. O. K. (2017). Learning to translate in real-time with neural machine translation. *ArXiv:1610.00388 [Cs]*. Retrieved from http://arxiv.org/abs/1610.00388.

16 Ma, M., Huang, L., Xiong, H., Zheng, R., Liu, K., Zheng, B., Zhang, C., He, Z., Liu, H., Li, X., Wu, H., & Wang, H. (2019). STACL: Simultaneous translation with implicit anticipation and controllable latency using prefix-to-prefix framework. *Proceedings of the 57th Annual Meeting of the Association for Computational Linguistics* (pp. 3025–3036). Retrieved from https://doi.org/10.18653/v1/P19-1289.

17 Colorín Colorado (2007, March 12). *Learning about your students' backgrounds* [Text]. Colorín Colorado. Retrieved from www.colorincolorado.org/article/learning-about-your-students-backgrounds.

18 Ma et al. (2019).

4

Empowering Students With Physical and Learning Challenges

There is another group of students who have disproportionately higher odds of not succeeding in their academic journey. They are students with physical and learning challenges.[1]

One sub-group: students with learning and attention challenges, like ADHD, dyslexia, and dysgraphia, need the world around them to understand the patterns of how their minds see and respond to things. Unfortunately, however, everything shaping the learning experience around them is often adapted to the average "abled" student, which is a teacher's guess of a middle ground of the abilities of the majority of students, rather than an actual medium-achieving student. Teachers struggle to identify patterns in the lives of students with challenges,[2] because to identify patterns one must have seen lots of the same kind of thing, over and over again. Even when teachers begin to identify these patterns, they get drowned out in the pressure

DOI: 10.4324/9781003183235-4

to produce instructional actions targeted at the needs emerging from patterns from the average "abled" students.

Similarly, students with physical impairments or imbalanced motor skills often get subjected to environments and social demands where they physically cannot respond at the capacity of their classmates. This time, it is the students that fail to see patterns that quickly.

But Can't Teachers Act, Watch, and Listen Differently to Support Them?

It's much easier said than done.
For starters, sharing just about any information with 25–40 children with varying learning needs and paces is already very complex. Now add to that the complexity of each student with a physical and learning disability needing information to be personalized and communicated slightly differently (through "accommodations," as they may be called), often without the help of special education support staff. This becomes even more complex when teachers are required to alter their teaching plans—the time, the materials, the goals for each task—for every student's success.

This is logistically hard and mentally exhausting on a teacher's part.[3] There are too many patterns and too much information for what a typical human brain is accustomed to processing.

So, what's our best solution when resources are available? Grouping all such students and sending them into special education programs. Granted, these have a few advantages, but are still a far cry from ideal because teachers constantly resort to finding common grounds even more within these more targeted groups of students. They still forcefully impose generalized patterns they find in a small subset of students with a wide range of challenges.

Essentially, Personalized Support Is Expensive and Inaccessible Because It Requires Too Many Trained People

And that reality helps us understand why existing special education programs all around the world are still inadequate in meeting the needs of students with challenges. Existing programs that individualize teaching and learning are a luxury,[4] and only a small minority of schools and school systems can go out of their way to provide such support of good quality.

The reality of most students with such challenges around the world is very dismal. Having several family members living with different physical and mental challenges that I struggle to understand, I know how inaccessible good support services are, primarily due to cost. This cost dynamic makes AI tools extremely lucrative for providing very individualized support because computers don't struggle with tirelessly making *predictions* for different *inputs* for different people.

A mind-boggling example of the number of people whose needs could be understood, albeit shallowly, in very little time is how search engines can respond to millions of people's wildly different queries every second. Search engines are also an extreme yet great example of how significant upfront human and financial investment into artificial intelligence can trickle down benefits to a large number of people for perpetuity, when created with the right and managed intentions.

Let's Continue With the Theme of AI Helping Students Perceive the World

One of the things we have spent time on is pattern recognition capabilities that help us read and listen to what students are saying and writing. We also discussed ways for students to hear us in their native language. What about their ability to see and hear the world when the world is far more complex than their senses can take in?

Let's consider a subset of sensory challenges that most severely affect students' abilities to engage with instruction: challenges in hearing, seeing, and expressing themselves.

New vocabulary	Some students with an auditory processing disorder are challenged from listening in on what teachers are saying.
	Teacher or peer speech can be captured through the same hardware improvements as student speech can, as we discussed earlier, and then used with *Automatic Speech Recognition*, supported by *models* using *RNNs*. Having words transcribed to a screen or available for playback after adjusting the frequency or pitch gives them multiple **modes** (i.e., in written and in audio) to process language. This screen could be on a hand-held pager-like device, on a tablet computer, or a wearable computer like special eyeglasses with text in subtitles—all with rewind and forward buttons.

What about visual impairments in perceiving the environment around them?

We discussed earlier how *deep learning* has helped read handwritten letters and words on scans of student responses to questions.

Just the way advancements in AI have made computers become good at reading text from still images, in the same way they can now see the world around them as a series of images stitched together. Images with things other than letters: people, objects, actions, gestures, and interactions between them. We can try and make *predictions* on all of these.

New vocabulary	*CNN-based deep learning models* have not just been a breakthrough in reading text, but in recognizing "things" (the word used for objects with well-defined shapes, including people) and "stuff" (arbitrary background regions)[5] in images in general. They can *predict* not just the likelihood of the presence of stuff and things in an image, but more crucially, they can be used with *classification* to tell us what thing is in a part of that image. Is it a pug or a chihuahua? Is it male or female?

Oh, never mind, that's actually a cupcake!

Given that we see multiple objects or people in an image, we can use *trained Natural Language Processing models* to *predict* words that describe relationships between the multiple things found in an image. Combining this with *language models* to construct sentences or phrasing that has the highest *prediction* of making sense, a process called **image captioning**, these sentences can begin to represent very meaningfully what's in the image.[6]

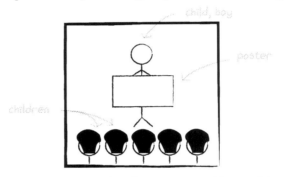

Attempt 1: child holds poster as children watch
Attempt 2: child shows poster as children watch
✓ Attempt 3: boy presents poster to children from front

FIGURE 4.1 A simple example of image captioning from objects identified and their placements in an image

When *trained* with a lot of *labeled* examples, such *models* can effectively caption images or video as they are seen.

As long as there is a sensor for capturing the world visually—like a camera—it has now become possible for the student wearing the device, like a headset or smart glass with a camera, to get this summary through text or speech played back to them through a pair of headphones or other technology that can send audio signal without blocking the ears.

Tool to try	Microsoft's Seeing AI ($$$) is an app that allows people with visual impairments to gain information about objects and spaces around them. It allows a visually impaired person to point the mobile phone camera at the scenery or a document or signboard in front of them and have it read back to them as speech.

In auditory or visual impairments, having AI hear and see the world for you is extremely useful. But what if the latter half of a student's perception is challenged, that is, the problem isn't with their sensory organs, and they can see and hear everything just fine, but just can't perceive them properly. An example of this is when a student feels challenged with decoding of text they read, while having perfect eyesight and hearing. Such decoding challenges come well before the student has a shot at grasping the meaning of the text.

New vocabulary	A key aspect of trying to figure out ways to make text more readable is focusing on diagnosing why a student struggles in the first place. Most reading teachers would at that point know what kind of intervention or scaffold can lower the sensory demand.
	So how might we diagnose the nature of the struggles? What signals can we capture so that we can use *machine learning* to make *predictions*?
	With enough examples, a *logistic regression model* can either take audio or video *inputs* of students' facial expressions and read-alouds, converting them into mathematical representations like *matrices*, and try to *predict classes* of difficulty from verbal and nonverbal cues. Imagine these being captured through a class-wide camera that focuses on the student during whole-group reading sessions, or small independent desk cameras that can be turned on only for reading sessions, which communicate with the teacher's device.
	This will *predict* the nature of the difficulty and the places where it occurred.

The ability to "see" their surroundings through text and audio does not just support students with visual impairments, but also engages multiple senses of students with learning challenges who—like in the case of dyslexia—might not be able to follow written text easily, or in the case of autism spectrum disorders, might struggle to perceive emotions of other people.

But learning is a more complex process; merely knowing where the students are struggling in their perception does not offer opportunities to remediate the learning moment. This goes beyond students with specific learning challenges. What we really need is something akin to a check for understanding, where AI can gauge the quality of the perception and the quality of the reproduction or internal synthesis of a newly acquired skill or piece of content for students of all learning capacities.

Our goal should be to go beyond the low-hanging fruits of student regurgitation through trial-and-error if we want to gauge perception and quality of reproduction. Any new learning that doesn't pass through working memory, and doesn't require transfer of an understanding and application into a new context, interferes with a student opportunity to exercise and exhibit his/her full learning capacities.

There is one such non-shallow way to gauge learning challenges and check for understanding of a newly acquired piece of content that we know can be reproduced in, very often, only one right way. That is through learning how to read and speak new vocabulary in a foreign language. Not only do a large number of languages have sounds not present in other major languages of the world, sometimes, even when written in the Latin alphabet, but also letter combinations in different languages are pronounced differently.

New vocabulary	The techniques in *machine learning* focused on "listening" to the student, determining how well or poorly the word or phrase was spoken, and then providing remediation for addressing the specific issue, is called **mispronunciation detection and diagnosis**.[7]
	Based on the most reliable ways to do this, the first step in the process is to use the same *models* as used in *Automatic Speech Recognition (ASR)*. In the process of *predicting* intended words, a good *ASR model* first *predicts* individual phonemes that have been uttered. *Mispronunciation detection and diagnosis* systems can compare spoken phonemes to expected phonemes, from knowledge of the words it is prompting the student to read, and consequently stress which phonemes need to be remediated.
	What makes this a tricky process is that when learning a foreign language, a language learner's pronunciations are often not wrong in their first language or accent.
	This is solved by *training* an *ASR model* on lots of data of speakers whose foreign languages are different from the ones they are currently learning.

Tool to try	Google's Read Along ($$$) is an Android app that listens to students read story books and gives positive rewards on good reading and provides feedback on mispronounced words.

The other side of being assisted in engaging with the world, and specifically the learning environments around them, is being able to participate.

Beginning With the Ability to Speak

The ability to "speak" fluently goes beyond helping those without a literal voice; computers that assist in the process are invaluable tools for students who struggle to vocalize their thoughts with confidence—which used to be some part of most of us growing up. Technologies as commonplace as microphones and amplifiers that magnify human voice and offer the chance for people without loud projections to be heard, make them an invaluable part of our current lives. And assistive reading devices and screen readers allow people without a voice to put their ideas out into the world.

Yet, so far, we have primarily only been talking about AI that reads and sees the world, because it tries to see patterns in signals other people or things give. But with the *NLP* examples in this chapter, we already began exploring another side of AI—one where AI can produce signals for the rest of the world. Coherent signals, which are sometimes produced by putting together lots of *predictions* we think work together.

Using *deep learning*, which gives us powerful tools to make *predictions* about the most likely patterns, and advancements in *NLP*, we can begin to talk about one of the greatest feats in AI thus far: **producing human-like speech.**

New vocabulary	Computers creating speech audio is called **Speech Synthesis**.[8]
	They do this either on human-authored text, such as reading a novel, or computer-generated sentences. The sub-field of *NLP* focused on computers constructing human-understandable phrases and sentences is called **Natural Language Generation (NLG)**.[9]
	Just like with *Automatic Speech Recognition* and *machine translation*, researchers tried to solve *Speech Synthesis* too without *deep learning* for a very long time. Using innovative *neural network* architectures harnessing the *sequence-to-sequence* idea and lots of examples, scientists have made extremely promising strides in converting text into speech in recent years.
	For example, in some recent successful architectures, these *models* convert graphemes to phonemes, and *predict* the best duration and frequency of segments of the generated sentences. (If you aren't familiar with graphemes and phonemes, a Google search might very quickly take you to a kindergarten reading lesson.)

> When discussing making *predictions* earlier, we always treated a *prediction* to be a number, a *class* associated with a number, or words again associated with certain numbers. In *Speech Synthesis*, series of bite-sized sounds, units of spectra of frequencies called **spectrograms**, and their sequences, all represented mathematically as a bunch of numbers, are *predicted*. So, we can now go from a bunch of numbers as *inputs* to *predicting* a bunch of numbers as the *output*.
>
> These predicted *spectrograms* can be saved as audio files and played back on any computer device just as MP3 files can. Except this time, you hear human-like speech which is sometimes indistinguishable from audio that wasn't generated by the computer.

> *Data hunger*
>
>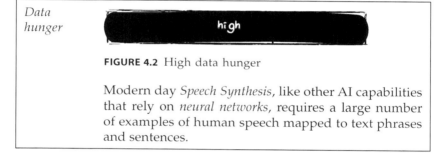
>
> **FIGURE 4.2** High data hunger
>
> Modern day *Speech Synthesis*, like other AI capabilities that rely on *neural networks*, requires a large number of examples of human speech mapped to text phrases and sentences.

I have a feeling that the first thing that came to your mind when we started discussing *Speech Synthesis* is that robotic sound of computers talking; the Stephen Hawking kind. Fortunately, the recent advances in AI changed that. After initial hiccups, *deep learning*-based techniques have made significant strides in producing audio that sounds very natural and expressive. This has resulted in so many devices around you that have an expressive human AI that can speak to you.

> *Tool to try*   Amazon (AWS) Polly ($$$) is a tool that "synthesizes" text you provide into very human-like speech. Tools from Google, Microsoft, and many other Speech Synthesis providers offer such capabilities with a large number of voices and accents.

Empowering Students ◆ 81

But nonetheless, there is something artificial-sounding about it. A 7-year-old male child with speech impairment connected to a system that synthesizes speech that sounds like a 36-year-old woman just doesn't make any sense. We really want AI that sounds like the person who we are giving a voice to.

New vocabulary	For a large amount of historical work into *Speech Synthesis* technologies, the goal was to be able to get just any good sounding voice from it.
	Synthesized or generated audio from these systems often sounded like your high-school debate champion with that oh-so-perfect voice! And that's because it was produced by *models trained* on examples of a single hand-picked human who probably came to a sound recording studio for weeks to record her voice samples. And that was the data the *neural networks trained* on— with the pre-written sentence as the *input*, and the audio produced by the human "expert" as the *output*.
	Historically, the *model* could produce sound like whoever's voice data we could procure a reasonable amount of, because we needed to *train* a *model* from entirely new data. But in recent years, we have begun to get past this limitation, with *deep learning* research increasingly focusing on **multi-speaker** *models*.[10]
	In fact, we don't even need that large an amount of new voice data to be able to build *models* that synthesize it. This is possible because of *models* learning to *predict* the differences in the voice textures of different humans, formally called **speaker adaptation**. And so, once a *model* has been *trained* on one human voice, it only needs to toggle some *coefficients* of some *functions* in the *neural network*—everything else works for all speakers. Because, at the end of the day, several physical properties of the way we speak are largely the same, as compared to the sounds created by, for example, a pigeon.
	This has also given rise to work in **voice cloning**,[11] which is an extension of the *speaker adaptation* idea where we can very quickly make the *model* generate the voice of a person who hasn't come to a recording studio to record a lot of their voice in perfect conditions, but there are enough recorded pieces of their voice which can be learned from.

> *Tool to try* Overdub ($$$) is an app that uses *deep learning* to allow anyone to make a digital version of their own voice with just a minute or so of *training* audio. This allows one to synthesize speech of a large piece of text without needing to narrate it painstakingly.

So yes, while we could be talking about giving that 7-year-old the voice of Morgan Freeman—let's not get carried away! An AI that speaks almost like the student means that it can "speak" like every other child. And if the impairment is psychological, hearing their thoughts vocalized can go a long way in giving students the confidence to speak independently, without coercion or pressure that we usually apply.

Where the Rubber Meets the Road

We've discussed AI enabling perception, and speech generation for students. We have been focusing on auditory and visual opportunities because these constitute the bulk of the sensory interaction in the teaching and learning process.

But discussing these in isolation from each other and in isolation of the grander context still leaves a lot to be desired. The bigger issue a lot of the students with physical and learning challenges face is **meaningful interaction** with teachers who can spend extensive amounts of time with them probing for understanding and interpreting their learning capacity or their "zone of proximal development."[12] A student's zone of proximal development is the range of knowledge and skills the student is close to being able to learn, given some help.

We discussed earlier that personalized attention was hard and extremely expensive. It should come as no surprise that the highest returns on any technology for this population of students will come from AI techniques that can vastly increase meaningful content interaction time through personalized scaffolding, something that is often very hard to do in large classrooms.

Let's see if we can find a way to amplify such student interaction with teaching/guidance and content.

New vocabulary	We briefly touched upon a sub-field of *NLP* called *Natural Language Generation* where techniques help generate new phrases and sentences based on some *classes predicted* in a picture. And in an earlier chapter we discussed another sub-field called *Natural Language Understanding* where the focus was to untangle phrases and sentences to extract some meaning from them.
	These advancements have led to a surge of progress in an important domain at the intersection of *NLP*, *Automatic Speech Recognition*, and *Speech Synthesis* called **Dialogue Systems**.[13]
	Whether or not speech recognition is used, *Dialogue Systems* are places where a computer can have a dialogue, or conversation, with a human in natural language. And not in clicks, menus, and pages.

It is one thing for a computer to hear you and read things to you. And a whole other to have a continuous conversation with you. That's because having a conversation involves remembering all the things someone said within the conversation and building up to a productive point which moves the understanding of all involved parties forward.

New vocabulary	In an earlier chapter, we discussed how making *predictions* on *Automatic Speech Recognition* was significantly improved by using the idea of *sequence-to-sequence* in *deep learning*.
	This indeed made a little bit of intuitive sense; we can *predict* one sequence of something (in this case, sound) to another sequence (of words in sentences). The *predictions* are better when we make them on the whole sequences because, for example, when we, as humans with our natural senses, miss or misunderstand words in a low-quality phone call, we are quickly able to guess what was said based on the rest of the sentence.

> This very same idea can be used in one primary *deep learning model* kind used in *Dialogue Systems* called (neural) **conversational models**. Such *models predict* follow-up statements in a natural conversation, thus allowing the computer to evaluate and generate potentially appropriate responses to a human "query." So, we just went from *prediction* based on a sequence of words, to *predictions* based on a sequence of statements in a conversation.
>
> At the time of this writing, we are still in the early days of *conversational models* having non-topic-specific open-ended conversations and general chit-chat (yes, that's the technical term for it) that help a human solve a particular problem. But a lot of exciting progress in this field gives us hope that machines will be capable of having human-like conversations with humans in the future.

Tool to try	Google Duplex ($$$) is a conversational *dialogue system* based in *deep learning* that allows restaurant and barber shop owners to set up an automated assistant to attend to appointment and order calls from customers. Duplex can understand questions asked by customers and use a synthesized voice and a *conversational model trained* to keep track of conversations and look up information from the store's schedule and menu of offerings in response to questions.

When it comes to teaching and learning, it becomes even more critical for such conversations to happen in a grounded understanding of the discipline associated with the goal of the discussion. These conversations wouldn't be very rich without these technologies knowing what they are talking about when it comes to the topics around which students with difficulties struggle.

While this specific scenario is unlikely to happen, just as an example, imagine if a student expressed confusion with figuring out a "part" in a middle school mathematics problem. The technology would never guess that the student was struggling with a fraction in the equation—since fractions are also called "parts"—but rather assume from simple knowledge of grammar that they are struggling with some piece of the exercise.

Sometimes, the words and phrases that constitute the conversation reflect the specific content in the curriculum, and other times they might very well reflect probing and motivation techniques from psychology, especially, but not limited to, early childhood development and mental wellness.

New vocabulary	So, now we are going from a general understanding of sentences and their connections with other sentences to trying to figure out what words and phrases in them truly mean. Having this understanding makes computers a whole lot smarter at being able to *predict* a better response or prompt sentence.
	First, computers need to identify specific keywords—often nouns and pronouns—in our sentences which will help it associate meaning around the rest of the conversations. Such keywords are called **entities** in the *NLP* world.[14]
	To do this, they depend on methods from a problem area known as **Named Entity Recognition** (NER),[15] and its sibling called **Entity Resolution**. These are methods of taking, sometimes ambiguous, words or phrases from a sentence and associating them with the meanings of entities from databases of things/people/places, and in our case, topics.
	But what does this database look like? Is it like a list of things on a spreadsheet?
	Well, it's a little more than that. To understand this database of sorts, we'd have to get our feet slightly wet in another crucial field within AI that *NLP* works closely with: **Knowledge Representation and Reasoning** (KRR).[16]
	So many acronyms! Don't worry, we will gradually learn more about this field, but for now are going to stick to one key concept from it. And that one key concept is a **knowledge graph** or **knowledge base**. A *knowledge graph* is like that database full of connected things/people/places/topics that are placed on what would look to us like a map of connected *entity* bubbles. These connections usually describe the relationship between any two entities.

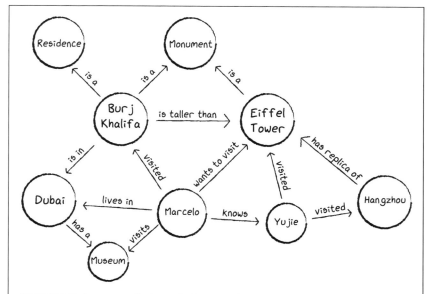

FIGURE 4.3 An example knowledge graph

So, if we made a *knowledge graph* on important personalities in our times, an entity on **Barack Obama** is connected to the entity on **Michelle L. Obama** with a connection that says: "spouse." Or just "bae."

When using the term *"knowledge base,"* though, it could look less like haphazard bubbles and more like a structured and sequenced list of things. Like a sequence of learning outcomes for a particular grade stored in **relational databases**—yes, the same stuff that holds most of the world's user information we see online.

Tool to try	Since finding *entities* using *NLP* and putting them into *knowledge graphs* are very technical tasks, tools in this world are mainly targeted at software programmers building specific apps for their audiences, which could be teaching and learning in some cases. You may try them out without needing to know how to program!
	IBM Watson's Natural Language tools ($$$) help extract *entities* and their relationships from a piece of text. Microsoft's Bing Entity Search ($$$) can "resolve" these *entities* and provide pictures and descriptions about the *entity*.

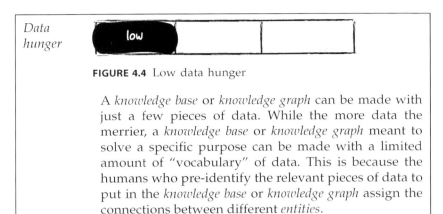

FIGURE 4.4 Low data hunger

A *knowledge base* or *knowledge graph* can be made with just a few pieces of data. While the more data the merrier, a *knowledge base* or *knowledge graph* meant to solve a specific purpose can be made with a limited amount of "vocabulary" of data. This is because the humans who pre-identify the relevant pieces of data to put in the *knowledge base* or *knowledge graph* assign the connections between different *entities*.

Recognizing topics and problems students are talking about—because we already have them in our *knowledge graphs*—changes computer statements from shallow questions about many things to more specific and targeted engagements and suggestions. This gives opportunities to capture where these students really are at in their emotional and knowledge development journey. The beginnings of meaningful interactions.

New vocabulary	The AI tools that generate new questions from a *knowledge graph* or *knowledge base* are called automatic **question generators**.[17]
	And *dialogue systems*, where meaningful questions are asked and answered based on knowledge, are often characterized as **question-answering systems**, that is, computer programs that answer our questions phrased in human language.

Tool to try	Maluuba (now Microsoft Research Montreal) was a *question-answering dialogue system* in the form of an app (called EpiReader) that could have a conversation and answer arbitrary questions from books. It demonstrated success with answering completely arbitrary questions about things in J.K. Rowling's "Harry Potter and the Philosopher's Stone."

Bringing It All Together

Probably the most exciting of all possibilities comes from being able to combine these technologies to engage all senses at once, by using cloned voice to engage with a student for a sustained period, all the while listening and "thoughtfully" responding to student speech, using knowledge of response profiles from having similar conversations with other students.

This idea has become more increasingly normalized in a world of conversational agents around us and in Hollywood movies. They allow us to imagine a future where we put humanness in taboo assistive technologies.

All that said, there are times when learning about a student does not happen by making them say something or using AI that produces sound on their behalf. These meaningful signals often take time to generate. To be able to understand any person with any difficulties, it isn't as easy to get much of an understanding from what they write or what they say as it is from **how they feel** and how they express that. And that's what we will talk about in the next chapter.

> The pinnacle of AI's greatness, as we define it today, will be when AI will turn into **AGI**—which stands for "Artificial General Intelligence"—or AI that can do everything a human can, but perhaps with several magnitudes more efficiency.[18]
>
> Generally, humans are known for being far more advanced than machines in their capabilities to empathize with others in particular situations. But this may not be true in all scenarios; as we have discussed earlier, the human mind is best trained to meet the needs of average "abled" people. Even trained professionals are limited to certain rules or patterns from their past experiences, when working with students with physical and learning challenges. It is quite possible that our inability to understand the needs of students very

different from the average is somehow rooted in the limitations of our complex biological neural networks.

I believe that this should push us to always consider an amended north star version for AI, beyond *AGI* as we currently know it—**an AGI that has the perception and empathizing capabilities humans wish to possess, but are unable to possess today, due to their own cognitive limitations.**

New classrooms	Every year, Ms. Wuku's students prepare for higher education or vocational careers in different parts of her country and internationally. In those places, her students' local dialect is not spoken. It's either a standardized English, Spanish, Hindi, Mandarin, Swahili, Farsi, or another major language. Ms. Wuku isn't proficient at the pronunciation in the major language either. Sometimes, these institutions require students to take oral language proficiency tests, like TOEFL or IELTS in the case of Western English.
	In the past, her poorer students were unfairly at a disadvantage because they could not afford language coaching. But now, Ms. Wuku can help her students practice. She offers one-on-one time for students in need of such help. She puts a piece of writing on the table and opens a pronunciation app on her basic smartphone to take a picture of it. After taking the picture, she presses the "record" button and keeps the phone on the table in front of the student. She asks the student to read the writing aloud. After the student completes the reading, the app highlights all the words where the student mispronounced the phonemes and offers corrective pronunciation.
	Ms. Wuku's students take standardized assessments at the end of the academic year. In Ms. Wuku's school, these assessments dictate a lot of practice and preparation of the content taught. But just like standardized

> assessments around the world, the body that conducts these assessments changes guidelines by a little bit every year. And every teacher subscribed to that assessment body is brimming with questions on what skills and content will be assessed. In the past, there has never been a proper answer to emails and calls requesting this clarity, because lots of teachers have lots of questions for a handful of assessment designers.
>
> Now, the assessment body started a website where any teacher can ask questions about how the skills and content in their syllabus for this academic year will be assessed. Ms. Wuku goes to the site and is greeted by a digital assistant. Ms. Wuku inquires about the length and depth of expected responses in a chat window in her natural language, gets immediate responses, and uses that knowledge to prepare students for the assessment.

Notes

1 Samuels, C. A. (2018, April 11). Scores stagnant for students with disabilities on "nation's report card." *Education Week*. Retrieved from www.edweek.org/teaching-learning/scores-stagnant-for-students-with-disabilities-on-nations-report-card/2018/04.
2 Rock, M. L., Gregg, M., Ellis, E., & Gable, R. A. (2008). REACH: A framework for differentiating classroom instruction. *Preventing School Failure*, 52(2), 31–47. Retrieved from https://0-www-proquest-com.www.saclibrarycatalog.org/scholarly-journals/reach-framework-differentiating-classroom/docview/228486162/se-2?accountid=4864.
3 Broderick, A., Mehta-Parekh, H., & Reid, D. K. (2005). Differentiating instruction for disabled students in inclusive classrooms. *Theory into Practice*, 44(3), 194–202. Retrieved from https://0-www-proquest-com.www.saclibrarycatalog.org/scholarly-journals/differentiating-instruction-disabled-students/docview/218800724/se-2?accountid=4864.

4 Peters, S. J. (2003). *Inclusive education: Achieving education for all by including those with disabilities and special education needs*. Washington, DC: World Bank Group. Retrieved from http://documents.worldbank.org/curated/en/614161468325299263/Inclusive-education-achieving-education-for-all-by-including-those-with-disabilities-and-special-education-needs.
5 Caesar, H., Uijlings, J., & Ferrari, V. (2018). Coco-stuff: Thing and stuff classes in context. *2018 IEEE/CVF Conference on Computer Vision and Pattern Recognition* (pp. 1209–1218). Retrieved from https://doi.org/10.1109/CVPR.2018.00132.
6 Hossain, M. Z., Sohel, F., Shiratuddin, M. F., & Laga, H. (2019). A comprehensive survey of deep learning for image captioning. *ACM Computing Surveys (CsUR)*, 51(6), 1–36.
7 Li, K., Qian, X., & Meng, H. (2016). Mispronunciation detection and diagnosis in l2 English speech using multidistribution deep neural networks. *IEEE/ACM Transactions on Audio, Speech, and Language Processing*, 25(1), 193–207.
8 Wang, Y., Skerry-Ryan, R. J., Stanton, D., Wu, Y., Weiss, R. J., Jaitly, N., ... & Saurous, R. A. (2017). Tacotron: Towards end-to-end speech synthesis. *Proceedings of Interspeech 2017* (pp. 4006–4010).
9 Gatt, A., & Krahmer, E. (2018). Survey of the state of the art in natural language generation: Core tasks, applications and evaluation. *Journal of Artificial Intelligence Research*, 61, 65–170.
10 Ping, W., Peng, K., Gibiansky, A., Arik, S. O., Kannan, A., Narang, S., Raiman, J., & Miller, J. (2018, February 15). Deep voice 3: Scaling text-to-speech with convolutional sequence learning. *International Conference on Learning Representations*. Retrieved from https://openreview.net/forum?id=HJtEm4p6Z.
11 Arik, S., Chen, J., Peng, K., Ping, W., & Zhou, Y. (2018). Neural voice cloning with a few samples. *Advances in Neural Information Processing Systems*. New York: Curran Associates, Inc.
12 Vygotsky, L. S. (1978). *Mind in society: The development of higher mental processes*. Cambridge, MA: Harvard University Press.
13 Chen, H., Liu, X., Yin, D., & Tang, J. (2017). A survey on dialogue systems: Recent advances and new frontiers. *ACM SIGKDD Explorations Newsletter*, 19(2), 25–35.

14 Sarawagi, S. (2008). *Information extraction*. Norwell, MA: Now Publishers Inc.
15 Lample, G., Ballesteros, M., Subramanian, S., Kawakami, K., & Dyer, C. (2016, June). Neural architectures for named entity recognition. In *Proceedings of the 2016 Conference of the North American Chapter of the Association for Computational Linguistics: Human Language Technologies* (pp. 260–270).
16 Brachman, R., Pagnucco, M., Levesque, H. (2004). *Knowledge representation and reasoning*. Germany: Elsevier Science.
17 Kurdi, G., Leo, J., Parsia, B., Sattler, U., & Al-Emari, S. (2020). A systematic review of automatic question generation for educational purposes. *International Journal of Artificial Intelligence in Education*, 30(1), 121–204.
18 Goertzel, B. (2014). Artificial general intelligence: Concept, state of the art, and future prospects. *Journal of Artificial General Intelligence*, 5(1), 1.

5

Behavior and Classroom Management

Teachers and scholars will often argue in favor of the advantages of students learning together in groups. I often do too. We do this especially when challenged by some who think that all learning can be personalized and supported by technology at home. But one disadvantage of learning in groups that we cannot easily fix is the disruption caused to one student's learning when another student doesn't feel like learning and inevitably shows his/her discomfort by disrupting others.

There are a wide range of such behaviors that we have come to deem as unacceptable in our classrooms. Managing these is brutally exhausting for teachers, but more importantly, they take away from vital learning opportunities.[1] Even though students often act out when they are overwhelmed or have a difficult time, disengagement or loss of learning time may not be normalized, especially for other students in these heterogeneous classrooms.

DOI: 10.4324/9781003183235-5

Gone unchecked for long, behavior issues have long-lasting negative consequences. But when they are in their earliest phases, they are easiest to solve.[2]

Catching Them Early

So, what we really need to perfect is the science of understanding our students' cognitive and emotional states at all times, as opposed to perfecting punishment, suspension, and detention policies. In the same way that, in an ideal world, anthropologists, sociologists, and economists come together with data to shape macroeconomic policy, we need systems that help us capture, synthesize, and constantly crunch our best data on what students are experiencing, so that we intervene when hope is in abundance. Tirelessly crunching data and *predicting* the near future is exactly what AI shines at.

Let's begin with something we are good at making *predictions* with: student speech. We have earlier discussed how *Automatic Speech Recognition* can help turn recordable sound into sentences. But unlike in the case of talking to a voice assistant, many students are often speaking one after another, and sometimes on top of each other, especially right before the classroom becomes a behavior management nightmare. This also prevents a computer from building an individual profile of sorts of things said that represent a state of student's thinking or emotions.

New vocabulary	One of the most popular kinds of audio recordings that people very often hire professional transcribers for are conversations, for example, interviews, or phone calls, or meetings, because just like classroom audio recordings, there are often more than two speakers involved. This makes it hard for someone reading a transcript from an *Automatic Speech Recognition* system to distinguish between the speakers, especially when people speak on top of each other, thereby making transcriptions much less useful.

> This has led to active progress over the past couple of decades in one specific area in *Automatic Speech Recognition*: separating one person's voice from another's, a subtopic formally known as **speaker diarization**.[3] It shouldn't be confused with a similar area called **speaker separation**—where the goal is to separate the speech from the background noise.
>
> The big idea behind mathematically distinguishing different speakers is to use certain features in the **articulation** of things said in the audio to *predict* the presence of multiple speakers and then keep a detailed tally.
>
> While many different approaches have been tried over time, *deep learning* has supported many novel ideas in doing this.
>
> This is similar to how we might interpret the presence of multiple speakers when blindfolded—by guessing the texture or frequency or another feature of the voices.

Tool to try	TeachFX is a web application that allows teachers and administrators to analyze the conversation between a teacher and the students during a class period. Specifically, using *speaker diarization*, the application separates teacher voice from student voice, thereby giving a fairly accurate picture of how much opportunity the teacher gave the students to engage orally.

Once a computer can distinguish between different students' speech and correlate it to data it has already built so far on the student, it is time to begin to *predict* what the student is really saying. And I mean beyond recognizing their words. I mean:

Beginning to Recognize Emotion or Sentiments

As humans, we tend to become particularly good at this in one-on-one conversations as we grow older; we catch the slightest hesitations or sarcasm in the voices of our co-workers, friends, spouses, and children. This helps us resolve critical issues before they escalate. It should come as no surprise to you that a lot of humans take too long and are often never able to express their grievances in words.

These are insights that are hardest for a teacher to capture, especially when we most often demand that students respond chorally to our questions. A repeatedly frustrated or aggressive student voice responding with answers in a whole-group discussion gets really easily drowned out, even when it may feel like the whole class contributed in unison.

New vocabulary	If you think about it, while some of us are better than others at figuring out the emotions in the voice of the people we are speaking with, we all make very subjective guesses on what the person might be feeling, because we perceive emotional signs differently.
	This makes the problem of **speech emotion recognition**[4]—recognizing a speaker's emotions from just sounds—a relatively difficult problem to solve, even after using *deep learning*. Because, as we have discussed before, building a *model* that can make *predictions*—at least when it comes to *supervised learning*—depends on data that is *labeled* from before, most likely by humans. But the data loses its integrity if it is based on several people's subjective opinions of emotions, possibly laden with biases.
	In the past, many systems would aim to *classify* the emotion of a piece of speech into what were known as the six major "Ekman" categories, named after the psychologist Paul Ekman, who first identified them.[5] These were: anger, disgust, fear, happiness, sadness, or surprise. But as we know, human emotion is more complex. You could feel multiple of these—or a very different feeling altogether that these don't capture. This has led to mechanisms to *label* and *predict* various aspects of emotion along continuous spectra, rather than hard *labels*. An example of this is attributing an emotion as 6 percent angry, 49 percent happy, and 12 percent courageous. Yes, courageous!

> Other novel approaches have helped make big strides. This includes using the transcriptions based on good *Automatic Speech Recognition* in combination with the speech and other information found in the sound, called **acoustic features**, to *predict* the emotion. The text from the transcriptions is useful because we can use *language models* that *predict* emotion for the word or phrases uttered by the human.
>
> Since emotions are a result of some underlying causes of a situation, another novelty has been to go further and *predict* the mood or traits (e.g., tiredness, illness, intoxication—this last one hopefully not in the case of children—etc.) to better understand what is influencing the emotion.

Tool to try	Behavior Signals ($$$) and IBM Watson Tone Analyzer ($$$) are two tools among many that are used by software programmers to make apps that can detect emotions from a piece of audio or microphone inputs.

Individual student speech, and subsequent *predictions* of emotions from it, are very useful. But probably the best source of information on what is happening socially and emotionally in classrooms, even more than speech or writing in student notebooks, is continuous video footage of the classroom.

No, we don't want to know that there are a bunch of students and a teacher walking around; we already know that! We want to know if there is either a behavior or another kind of disruption about to happen.

New vocabulary	Gladly, there is an important sub-field of AI dedicated to helping *predict* the visual world—in images, videos, and the kind of imagery produced by light and sound sensors that can "see" spaces. It's called **Computer Vision**.[6]

Computer Vision, often supported by *machine learning*, offers us plenty of techniques to derive meaning from video footage like recorded classroom spaces. Techniques from the obvious-sounding **facial recognition** and **video tracking**,[7] done with or without *deep learning*, give us a shot at isolating and observing individual students.

Expression of student engagement can be further understood through the physical actions and movements a student being tracked may be doing. Recognizing the physical actions—either granular ones or many smaller actions that make up a larger well-understood action—is known as **activity recognition**.[8]

Although these are still very early days, recent successes in *activity recognition* are based on *RNNs*, something we discussed earlier. Specifically, a kind known as **long short-term memory** (LSTM)[9] *networks*. These are especially good at holding onto information from *neural network functions* from prior examples in the data.

In the case of *activity recognition*, consider this made-up situation. Suppose the current movement of a student is of them turning around and speaking loudly. This is an *input*. Without *RNNs*, this activity would be *predicted* as a distraction. However, because *RNNs* store some knowledge about previous *inputs*, we know from previous video footage *input* that the student behind threw an object that hit the student who turned around. This kind of reaction is not disruption, but a reflex. Thus, a well-*trained activity recognition model* using *RNNs* will not *predict* the student turning around to be at fault for the disruption.

Tool to try	Clarifai ($$$) is a tool for software programmers that uses the newest advancements in *deep learning* to *predict* the presence of certain objects in images and *classify* them. It also has made great strides in *predicting* suspicious activity from CCTV footage of a shared or open space.

Tool to try	To eliminate uploaded spam, hateful, or inappropriate video content, Facebook uses activity recognition on videos to better classify the contents of the videos through an internal tool called Lumos ($$$).

You are possibly in one of two camps of people right now: you are either thinking "nice! Technology is advanced enough to track individual students, something that is difficult for a teacher to do" or you have begun to worry about this being like a surveillance recording system that is riddled with privacy issues. Hang in there—we will discuss this concern towards the end of the chapter.

Regardless, we could possibly somewhat justify this intrusion if we could go further than just being able to know where each student is and the physical actions they are taking. Because teachers are more likely to miss emotional aberrations than they are visual ones.

New vocabulary	Let us extend the ideas of *speech emotion recognition* with our newfound abilities to understand students from video. *Speech emotion recognition* may be categorized under a larger problem area called **affect detection**.[10]
	When used with *facial tracking* in *computer vision*, *affect detection* techniques for recognizing emotional states from facial expressions allow us to capture even more holistic sentiments expressed by a child at any time—is he or she frustrated or struggling? Or is that a face of productive readiness? Sentiments that speech alone cannot capture.
	Such techniques may use tools from *computer vision* to track edges/corners and other facial features and feed these as *inputs* to *supervised learning* CNN-based *models* to do *classification* into a bunch of known emotional states.
	Combining *predictions* from *affects* recognized through speech and video together may allow us to construct *models* with higher *accuracy* and lower *bias*. Models like this that combine multiple "*modes*" together to make better *predictions* are based on a set of *machine learning* techniques called **multimodal learning**.[11] This is different from the multimodal learning in education where students learn using different modalities.

> *Tool to try*   Affectiva ($$$) makes a set of tools for self-driving-car makers to detect the *affects*—both audio and visual—of the passengers during their interaction with the on-board conversational assistant. This is useful to assess the mood and gaze of the passenger to always ensure safety. This technology may be ready for classrooms in the future as well.

Often, students disengage because their teacher is unable to adapt to their learning needs. From a teacher's perspective, this is understandably much less trivial than it sounds.

But always having such rich information about what students individually and as a whole are experiencing cannot just help a teacher play counselor, but can also inform a teacher's choices of instructional activities.

Finding Out the Whole Story

These discrete *predictions* of emotions and actions, albeit very useful, don't always tell us the whole story.

How a student is feeling right now might often be tied to what happened two periods ago. And it will most likely affect their emotional state all day, or worse, over multiple days. As AI learns to think like humans, it is getting better at building a complex understanding which is a result of a series of events over a longer span of time.

Fortunately, making *predictions* based on various influencing factors has very much been important in *machine learning*. Let's consider some of these ideas with an example related to understanding student emotions.

If you taught the same students for, say, two years, you would easily be able to look at a grumpy student during your 10am session and say something along the lines of "there is a 60 percent chance this student will be a nuisance in the next period." This isn't as straightforward as it looks on the surface to most people. You are able to say this with a level of certainty because you have seen this student enough times in such a situation and have observed what happened in the following periods. This is the same reason why a substitute teacher can't just take over your class and understand your students in a short duration of time.

New vocabulary	Mathematically, we want a simple way to represent what your mind has observed and knows, to come up with such a *prediction*. We can use an idea in study of probability called the **Bayes Theorem** to think about this. This theorem, which is represented by a simple formula that uses basic multiplication and division,[12] allows us to estimate the likelihood of one event based on another event happening.
	You know certain things about what happens in the 3rd period. Specifically, you know:
	• At that point of the day, students who haven't had breakfast are thinking about lunch and beginning to need a break. So, say, you think there is a 20 percent chance that any student in the classroom will cause trouble.
	• And right now, you know the number of students in the classroom which look grumpy; you can see exactly 10 percent of students sulking or getting fidgety.
	• Lastly, you know that if a student causes trouble in the 3rd period, there was about a 30 percent chance they were grumpy around 10am. Because you know that many times, they act out because of another student bothering them in the moment.
	Using this information, you could have found how likely it is that a student will be disruptive in the next period, given that he/she was grumpy around 10am, using the *Bayes Theorem*. Plugging in the information,
	$$(0.30 \times 0.20) / 0.10 = 0.60$$
	… we find that there is a 60 percent likelihood that a student in the classroom will be disruptive in the next period.

Your understanding of a student's behavior in the next period isn't just based on his or her current "state"; it is based on your two years of experience of observing hundreds of socially and emotionally distraught students/situations. And that's a lot of states.

New vocabulary	One of the aspects of the example we have been discussing about student behavior is that it is based on us making *predictions* about things that happened over time. Specifically, we were making *predictions* based on a sequence of behavior events or states. A kind of AI *model* that shines at making *predictions* based on a sequence of states is a **Markov Model**. *Markov models* are typically not *neural network models*. They are simpler in nature and are based on conditional probabilities—a future state given some current state—like the kind we saw when discussing *Bayes Theorem*. You might wonder how these are different from *RNNs*, which we also claimed worked very well with making *predictions* on sequences. They key difference comes from the Markov-ian property that gives its name to *Markov models*. According to this property, for example, a behavior *prediction* is based on the last known/observed behavior of the student. And nothing before that. In *RNNs*, as you may remember, we could hold onto information of many prior *inputs*. In our example, that means that an *RNN model* would use behavior states of students throughout the day, while a *Markov Model* would only use the very last behavior state, or what happened last period, to *predict* this period's behavior.
Data hunger	medium **FIGURE 5.1** Medium data hunger Because of the Markov property, *Markov models* are typically simpler than *neural networks*, for example, *RNNs*, and can often be made well with not as much data as *neural networks* require.

But you are probably skeptical here. You know that emotional states are complex, and it isn't always easy to make a *prediction* on how grumpy or inattentive a student will be based on their current behavior, especially when the students are different.

More importantly, at this stage, you are probably asking: why should we care about trying to *predict* a behavioral problem? So that we can give the student a warning or move their desk? No. We should care about this because there is an underlying learning or personal difficulty that we need to remedy as soon as possible. The behavioral acting outs are just a representation for the deeper issue at hand.

New vocabulary	These events are still occurring over time in a sequence. The only catch is that instead of focusing on *predicting* a behavioral problem, we wish to *predict* and anticipate the underlying learning or personal difficulty.
	A **Hidden Markov Model**[13] is a kind of *Markov Model* that makes *predictions* about an underlying likelihood that we can't easily observe—like in our case, a learning or personal difficulty—based on something we can indeed observe over time, like behavioral problems. And because it is a *Markov Model*, it also follows the principle of states occurring in a sequence.
	In these *models*, to make a *prediction* about a learning or personal difficulty, using a specific probability formula, we'd need to know the probabilities of going from one state of student behavior to another. For example, we'd need to know the likelihood of a student being angry in one period to being disengaged in the next period, or enthusiastic in one, too tired in the next. You get the point.
	We'd also need to know the likelihood or probability of common behavior problems given certain learning or personal difficulties. For example, we'd need to know that if a student is disturbing their neighbor, how likely it is that the student is unable to engage with the material being taught.
	As a side note: before *deep learning models* became popular, popular *machine learning* problems like *Automatic Speech Recognition* were, and in some places still are, solved with *Hidden Markov Models*.

This ability to make *predictions* on emotions and learning difficulties more confidently with more information, but to also shine in the absence of enough examples of similar anomalies in behavior, can prove to be highly useful for even the most attentive teacher.

By AI, but Only for the Teacher

> As noted earlier, reflecting on these opportunities of understanding students through video observations in the classrooms in large numbers can very easily ignite pop-culture-inspired horrors of ethical catastrophes and mass surveillance. But that fear comes from the invalid assumption that the only way to use the knowledge generated from the AI is through centralized systems either making decisions themselves or enabling supposed cold and heartless administrators who don't know these kids to decide their fate.
>
> **At least until now**
>
> In reality, for sensitive information, like video footage of classrooms that can be critical to improving behavior, none of these videos need to be stored centrally. Have you heard about your smartphone camera using AI without your pictures ever leaving your phone? These are the very same technological advancements that allow us to build systems that do not upload or store video to be retrieved later. They "see" the students using a camera (just like a teacher sees her students), a *prediction* is made, and then that footage is deleted.
>
> In other cases, video that is centrally stored temporarily is accessed under meticulously drafted and enforced ethical use policies that everyone can agree is helpful and not harmful; for example, parents being able to keep an eye on their little child's well-being after leaving them at a day care facility.
>
> Nevertheless, there is no guarantee that the technology provider your school will use in the coming decade for such a capability will be responsible and ethically conscious. It's quite possible that

> the technology provider will attempt to justify the murky use of such information through allusions to means that "improve the system." This is yet another reason why it is even more important that educators are a crucial partner in the design of these technologies, and proper policy safeguards are put in place.

So far, we have seen quite a few examples on how data produced by students can be used to make *predictions*. In this chapter, as we began to make *predictions* on behavior, we naturally became a little uneasy about the ethics around collecting and storing this data. And on a similar note, I am guessing that at the back of your mind, during this entire process, there was a lingering question of: "how can I, as a teacher or administrator, begin to engage with this data and these *predictions*?" Undoubtedly, we need systems that manage and help us understand *predictions* made on individualized student learning, and help us protect student data while at it.

New vocabulary	The field at the intersection of AI and learning that focuses on the mechanisms and systems to "measure, collect, analyze, and report data about learners and their contexts, for purposes of understanding and optimizing learning and the environments in which it occurs"[14] is called **learning analytics**.
	Although still in their early stages of development, technological systems that will emerge from this field may give teachers access to this analysis to support and augment their day-to-day educational decision-making, such as the *predictions* made on student performance, attendance, and engagement. These *predictions* may be based on data that is captured from the "digital traces" students leave in interacting with technology primarily focused on learning. Additionally, such systems should aim to allow you to take control of policies and data that are critical to protecting your students.

Learning analytics' explicit focus on improving learning using *predictions* makes progress in the field more urgent than general AI systems made to solve a large variety of problems.

Given our emphasis on *screen-less* classroom environments, you are probably wondering what the usefulness of *learning analytics* is beyond classrooms where students constantly engage with computers that generate such data. Interestingly, even in schools where computing technology is an integral part of engaging students, a significant portion of learning takes place outside digital environments.[15]

New vocabulary	While most of the effort in *learning analytics* thus far has focused on data generated by students interacting with computers, there is an emerging sub-field called **Multimodal Learning Analytics** which grows the scope of the field to include sensing technologies that capture a large amount of data in physical spaces.
	Let's dissect the word "multimodal" here, since we have used it before too. "Multimodal" essentially means multiple modalities and modes.[16] Modality has been defined[17] as "the type of communication channel used to convey or acquire information," while mode has been defined as "a state that determines the way information is interpreted to extract or convey meaning." Therefore, "multimodal" extends the sources of learning data to come from anything that can be experienced by the five human senses or produced through modalities like speech, sound, gestures, and written work.
	A lot of the things we have been discussing until now revolve around supporting teachers with AI *predictions* made on classroom data not captured in digital traces. Capturing and analyzing this data is at the heart of *multimodal learning analytics*.

> Apart from data based on such modalities and *modes* that can be non-intrusively captured in classrooms around the world, the kinds of novel data that can be captured in this field through measured and controlled research in laboratories is large. These kinds of data may include data from "wearable cameras, wearable sensors, biosensors (e.g., that permit measurements of skin conductivity, heartbeat, and electroencephalography), gesture sensing, infrared imaging, and eye tracking."[18]

With *multimodal learning analytics*, a teacher can have insight into students' learning experiences beyond data captured in exercises, homeworks, and assessments assigned digitally. Such insight might include analysis from student behavior, participation with peers, student voice, effort, emotional states, and health and well-being, to name a few.

At the same time, with the emphasis on *multimodal learning analytics* in the domain of *learning analytics*, the systems available to schools and teachers that will emerge from this field will likely put emphasis on the ability for educators to control the parameters of when and how all this rich data, from digital and non-digital traces, is captured. For example, they may give teachers and administrators the control to limit access of behavior observations to only the teacher in the classroom for the duration of the period or for the rest of the day.

New vocabulary	A subset of *learning analytics*, or sometimes considered a closely related concept[19] (Elias, 2011), that "focuses on developing and implementing methods with a goal of promoting discoveries from data in educational settings"[20] is called **educational data mining**.
	While *learning analytics* and *educational data mining* are similar in their objectives, *educational data mining*'s focus is far more specific to possibilities with data than that of *learning analytics*, which is more concerned with user-friendly technologies that engage and inform the teacher. *Educational data mining* is focused on automatically finding insights from learning data, while *learning analytics* puts more emphasis on leveraging the judgment of educators.[21]

Tool to try	Acrobatiq ($$$) is a *learning analytics* product (originally tied to Carnegie Mellon University's Online Learning Initiative) that provides teachers and instructional designers with many insights about student interaction and progress. Currently, it is tied to students using computers as a part of their learning process, but this data can come from a classroom without a screen in front of every student.

Regardless of whether AI is used or not, if appropriate individual disciplinary interventions are made with the student at the right time, building months' worth of historical data on behavior issues is unnecessary. There are plenty of journals in schools around the world archiving disciplinary issues and consequent punishments of students, but there are far too few appropriate and considerate interventions that result in marked improvements.

Tool to try	While this is not a tool you can try, it's an example of something that has been implemented that applies *video tracking* to correctly *predict* a behavioral problem in the healthcare field, all while being sensitive to privacy concerns. A study conducted by medical and computer science faculty and students at Stanford University used data from imaging sensors in hospital room doorways in *neural networks* to *predict* "use and non-use of hand sanitizers, an important driver of patient safety,"[22] at greater than 95 percent accuracy. This was an extremely important piece of work because preventable bedside medical errors have harmed many patients for a long time. As far as privacy is concerned, "the team used depth and thermal sensors to create images of human shapes in motion without revealing their identity." This didn't involve the use of recorded video footage that a bad actor could misuse.

New classrooms	Ms. Wuku's class period is sometimes right after the physical education period. The physical education teacher used to share with Ms. Wuku how he wants to allow students to pick their sport or activity of choice, but it would be impossible to adequately support students in different spaces like courts, gyms, and fields far from one another.
	This problem has been solved today. The school installed cameras in each of the physical education spaces. The centralized computer connected to these cameras keeps a track of which students are participating in which sports and summarizes these statistics week-over-week for the teacher. Moreover, the physical education teacher has an app on a tablet that keeps track of what drills and tasks students are doing in each of these spaces. For example, when looking at data and footage from the volleyball court, he can monitor which students are spending how much time on warm up, shuffling positions, tossing serves, and putting the ball in motion. He has analytics like the kind professional sports teams gather with teams of analysts watching footage.
	In the past, Ms. Wuku really struggled to monitor how harmonious and collaborative students were in small-group discussions. While she enjoyed using the hand-sized microphone devices in each of the groups, the transcript didn't really help her to understand what students were feeling in conversation with their peers.
	Now, a newer version of the microphone devices has a 360-degree camera. It uses the audio from the microphone and footage from the device to determine the emotions of students speaking and detects conflicts, resentment, and disengagement, which didn't get expressed with words in the past. It shows all this information right on the teacher's tablet or computer, and she is able to mitigate bigger issues.
	Ms. Wuku cares a lot about her students' success and has always been generally aware of which students are higher performers and which students perform poorly.

> However, that care and concern hasn't always helped her change her instruction to improve learning outcomes for everyone in her classroom. She tried offering remedial classes, but as is the case with every other intervention which takes effort, it wasn't clear how helpful that was.
>
> Now, things look a lot different. Her school has adopted a practice to record all summative and formative assessment data digitally on a central student roster. With the introduction of devices that scan, read, and interpret daily student checks for understanding, and hand-sized microphone devices that track speech and participation in small-group work, there is plenty of data on each student. So, at the end of every school day, Ms. Wuku spends ten minutes on her laptop reviewing a high-quality online dashboard which has access to both the assessment data, and the speech and participation data from the classroom. This dashboard shows learning summaries and trajectories of students over any duration she wants. She can now pick the class period in which she tried something different in her instructional practice and run a report to see how significant an impact that change had compared to what she was doing in the past.

Notes

1 Beaman, R., Wheldall, K., & Kemp, C. (2007). Recent research on troublesome classroom behaviour: A review. *Australasian Journal of Special Education*, 31(1), 45–60.
2 Rogers, B. (2015). *Classroom behaviour: A practical guide to effective teaching, behaviour management and colleague support*. London: SAGE Publications.
3 Anguera, X., Bozonnet, S., Evans, N., Fredouille, C., Friedland, G., & Vinyals, O. (2012). Speaker diarization: A review of recent research. *IEEE Transactions on Audio, Speech, and Language Processing*, 20(2), 356–370.

4 Schuller, B. W. (2018). Speech emotion recognition: Two decades in a nutshell, benchmarks, and ongoing trends. *Communications of the ACM*, 61(5), 90–99.
5 Emotion classification. (2021). In *Wikipedia*. Retrieved from https://en.wikipedia.org/w/index.php?title=Emotion_classification&oldid=1003462771.
6 Russell, S., & Norvig, P. (2020). *Artificial intelligence: A modern approach* (4th edn). London: Pearson.
7 Wang, L., Liu, T., Wang, G., Chan, K. L., & Yang, Q. (2015). Video tracking using learned hierarchical features. *IEEE Transactions on Image Processing*, 24(4), 1424–1435.
8 Vrigkas, M., Nikou, C., & Kakadiaris, I. A. (2015). A review of human activity recognition methods. *Frontiers in Robotics and AI*, 2, 28.
9 Hochreiter, S., & Schmidhuber, J. (1997). Long short-term memory. *Neural Computation*, 9(8), 1735–1780.
10 Calvo, R. A., & D'Mello, S. (2010). Affect detection: An interdisciplinary review of models, methods, and their applications. *IEEE Transactions on Affective Computing*, 1(1), 18–37.
11 Ngiam, J., Khosla, A., Kim, M., Nam, J., Lee, H., & Ng, A. Y. (2011, January). Multimodal deep learning. *International Conference on Machine Learning*.
12 The probability of A happening given B happened can be calculated as: (probability of A happening × probability of B happening given A happened)/probability of B happening.
13 Rabiner, L., & Juang, B. (1986). An introduction to hidden Markov models. *IEEE ASSP Magazine*, 3(1), 4–16.
14 New definition of "learning analytics" presented by Society for Learning Analytics Research (SOLAR) at *First Learning Analytics and Knowledge Conference* in 2011.
15 Pardo, A., & Kloos, C. D. (2011). Stepping out of the box: Towards analytics outside the learning management system. *Proceedings of the 1st International Conference on Learning Analytics and Knowledge—LAK '11*, 163. https://doi.org/10.1145/2090116.2090142.
16 *Introduction to multimodal learning analytics—LearnAITech* (n.d.). Retrieved February 4, 2021 from https://learnaitech.com/introduction-to-multimodal-learning-analytics/

17 Nigay, L., & Coutaz, J. (1993). A design space for multimodal systems: Concurrent processing and data fusion. *Proceedings of the INTERACT '93 and CHI '93 Conference on Human Factors in Computing Systems* (pp. 172–178). https://doi.org/10.1145/169059.169143.
18 Blikstein, P., & Worsley, M. (2016). Multimodal learning analytics and education data mining: Using computational technologies to measure complex learning tasks. *Journal of Learning Analytics*, 3(2), 220–238.
19 Elias, T. (2011). *Learning analytics: Definitions, processes and potential.* Retrieved September 26, 2021 from: https://landing.athabascau.ca/file/download/43713; Bienkowski, M., Feng, M., & Means, B. (2012). *Enhancing teaching and learning through educational data mining and learning analytics: An issue brief.* Office of Educational Technology, US Department of Education. https://eric.ed.gov/?id=ED611199.
20 Nunn, S., Avella, J. T., Kanai, T., & Kebritchi, M. (2016). Learning analytics methods, benefits, and challenges in higher education: A systematic literature review. *Online Learning*, 20(2). Retrieved from https://doi.org/10.24059/olj.v20i2.790.
21 Siemens, G., & Baker, R. S. J. d. (2012). Learning analytics and educational data mining: Towards communication and collaboration. *Proceedings of the 2nd International Conference on Learning Analytics and Knowledge—LAK '12*, 252. Retrieved from https://doi.org/10.1145/2330601.2330661.
22 Digitale, E. (2018, April 10). *Researchers improve patient safety with bedside computer vision.* Stanford, CA: Stanford School of Engineering. Retrieved from https://engineering.stanford.edu/magazine/article/researchers-improve-patient-safety-bedside-computer-vision.

6

Curriculum Development and Alignment

Understanding students and helping students access a teacher's instructions with the help of AI is all well and good. But the learning is often only as good as the curriculum—the essential knowledge that we are trying to teach students in the first place. Any support and relief in developing curriculum will truly transform everything that happens before the bell rings for the classes.

But there is a good chance you are skeptical when it comes to AI's ability to develop curriculum even partially. Your argument against it most likely sounds like: curriculum needs to be designed, and it is an art that can only be mastered after years in the classroom observing how students react to different content and instruction.

DOI: 10.4324/9781003183235-6

Curriculum Development Is Both an Art and a Science

Curriculum development is indeed a creative endeavor, but only partially. Any good curriculum developer will tell you that there are several logical steps that need to be in place before plugging in some very-human creativity.

Curriculum that doesn't logically build on prior knowledge, logically drive towards predetermined learning outcomes, and/or factually represent the depth of the content to be taught cannot possibly be any good. While AI is advancing in its capability to learn what it means to be creative, it can make high-quality *predictions* and compose aspects of curriculum purely based on logical reasoning if it is *trained* with all critical pieces of data.

So, let's focus on that scientific aspect of curriculum development. Just like we have done before, let's try to dissect different aspects of what humans would usually do, so that we can try to map these abilities to some of AI's *prediction*-making capabilities. Brace yourself because this is going to be the most involved discussion we have had so far.

Let's break down the curriculum development process into these three main steps:

1. Understanding of content or knowledge in the domain.
2. Determining how to meet learning outcomes.
3. Generating and identifying teachable materials.

The final step, "Generating and identifying teachable materials" is split into the two parts, (a) Consumable knowledge, and (b) Assessment for learning.

Understanding of Content or Knowledge in the Domain

This is the first step in the three-step curriculum development process. Understanding of content accurately, for humans or AI, depends on canonical sources of accurate facts. Unfortunately, hidden inside and around our textbooks and online encyclopedias are some falsehoods pretending to be facts. For example, the Encyclopædia Britannica, a text which is widely regarded as a source of accurate general knowledge, used to state that water is colorless. This is probably what you learned in school as well. It turns out that water has an intrinsic blueish color,[1] but perhaps not as blue as every child's drawing you have seen so far. Until we have such 100 percent accurate sources, we must use what we have.

Apart from accuracy, we have another problem that needs solving to make AI useful: reconciling different representations of knowledge. By different representations of knowledge, I mean textbooks, learning progressions or suggested sequences, articles, supplementary teaching guides, words uttered in video and audio of interviews, personal accounts, talks, etc. These include all the things that signal to us: "these are the most important pieces of knowledge and this is the order and manner in which it may be understood." By "reconciling," I mean merging and synthesizing that knowledge.

Such reconciliation can be rather easy for a trained human. The more a human learns, the more proficient they become at organizing seemingly disconnected ideas and topics without being explicitly taught how to draw these connections. They become good at learning how to learn, and how to navigate an abundance of knowledge sources.

AI will eventually have this level of proficiency across domains of knowledge. But when presented with anything more complex than simple facts today, it depends on a little handholding to construct knowledge.

New vocabulary	Computers use their bits and bytes to construct knowledge, enabling themselves to memorize and store information much faster and in larger quantities than humans.

> The study and practice of extracting knowledge from documented materials like textbooks, encyclopedias, documentaries, journals, etc. is called **knowledge extraction**,[2] building on its little sibling **information extraction**, which uses many techniques from previously discussed *Natural Language Processing* and *Knowledge Representation and Reasoning* ideas.
>
> *Knowledge extraction* techniques help us make **knowledge representations**[3] like *knowledge bases/ knowledge graphs*, things we talked about earlier. Of course, these *representations* can also be manually made by an expert. Nevertheless, these *representations* here just mean the ways of organizing knowledge such that a computer understands and can work with it; like how humans organize knowledge in libraries in a certain disciplined manner.
>
> More formally, when there is an underlying language and vocabulary describing relationships between things in these *representations*, they are called **semantic networks**.[4] Such *representations* can eventually be used to reason about the knowledge, which we need to use in figuring out how to sequence curricular experiences.

Once computers can digest facts and turn them into knowledge or use existing synthesized knowledge in different forms and store them, we can begin to explore how these computers find out the pieces of knowledge that a particular piece of knowledge builds towards, and how it should be presented to humans.

Determining How to Meet Learning Outcomes

This is the second step in the three-step curriculum development process that I recognized earlier. In our traditional view of curriculum development, both outcomes, and the means to achieving them, are static. By "static," I mean they don't change once a course begins. Ideally, a teacher does not lower the difficulty level or change the depth and breadth of content that students need to master. In fewer cases, they may have to change these if students fall behind or school schedules demand it.

It makes all the sense for outcomes to be static. Having moving targets is a recipe for failure. Without it, the validity and integrity of the course would be questionable.

That said, the means to achieving these outcomes doesn't always have to be static. That's because the world is always changing and what works in one classroom at one time doesn't always work in another. More importantly, it's unlikely that a teacher's chosen progression and pedagogical choices are always the most optimal ones for helping all students succeed, since that requires high levels of expertise and research. In other words, it is likely that there is room for doing even better.

And so, while it would be ideal to change the means to achieving these outcomes based on a changing world, as well as on the changing needs of students, it is very difficult for teachers to constantly iterate on their lesson and unit progressions. This difficulty allows us to open ourselves up to the idea that AI could come up with these progressions more efficiently, so that teachers are not always stuck with predetermined and unchangeable means to achieving the outcomes, especially when it is not helpful for anyone.

New vocabulary	We discussed how computers store knowledge through *knowledge representations*. And in a previous chapter, we also discussed that people or places or things in such *representations* could be called *entities*.
	Just like an *entity*, we need a way to store something that is "learnable"—a way of saying something that a machine could potentially make *predictions* on—in a *knowledge representation*, to be able to reason about it and whether or not a student knows it. For example, while *Barack Obama* is an *entity*, "Barack Obama's presidential term," "how Barack Obama defended civil rights," "reasons for Barack Obama's successful wins" are all things students can learn and be competent at, resulting in the potential learning outcome we wish students to achieve.

> These "concept(s), principle(s), fact(s), or skill(s) ... misconception(s), or facet(s)"[5] are called **knowledge components**. A concept—for example, gravitation—can be a *knowledge component*. And so can a principle, like any theorem or a law of motion. *Knowledge components* can be made from facts, like the periodic table symbol for an element. And they can also be made from skills, like the ability to draw a velocity–time graph. A misconception, for example, weight being the same as mass, could be a suitable *knowledge component*. And even a *facet*, like the classification of a plant species, would make for a worthy *knowledge component*.
>
> While the term *knowledge component* is very popular in the world of *Intelligent Tutoring Systems*, I am going to substitute it with the word **competencies** for the rest of our discussion. Sometimes, these are formalized as state or national standards and are adopted by schools or just written out within a school or school district as learning outcomes. While all of these have slightly different official meanings, especially when it comes to who you ask and how they are used in practice, *competencies* are both teacher-friendly and a happy medium between them.

Selecting the *competencies* to target in students' educational experiences is a complex social process based on an ever-changing world, opinions, philosophies, human expertise, and constant learning research findings. And that's why AI doesn't get a shot at building them today, although one day it might very well do this.

So, which *competencies* are important and need to be learned are determined by humans. That said, there is a lot of room for AI to improve the sequence and specific curricular and instructional experiences—basically strategies, activities, quiz questions, readings, etc.—for meeting these *competencies* for, say, a particular grade level.

Curriculum Development and Alignment ◆ 119

New vocabulary

There are two ways to figure out what sequence of which specific curricular and instructional experiences will most optimally help us meet a given desired *competency*. These two can either be used exclusively, or in combination with one another.

The first is teacher-driven, or expert-driven, as experienced teachers would be called **experts** in our scenario. The idea is to populate what's called an **expert system**.[6] An *expert system* is mostly a non-mathematical kind of AI system that may be designed to make a computer think and reason about a situation or task similar to how a human mind might have thought and reasoned about it. It is specifically called an *"expert" system* because it is a computer system fed with facts and decision-making pathways learned from one or more experts in that specific field. It is fed this information after analyzing either their recorded knowledge of problem-solving and organization of many things, ideas, and explanations in their specific world, or by running experiments to study their thinking.

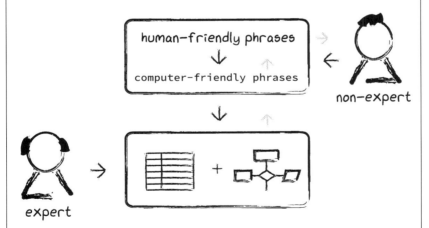

FIGURE 6.1 A simplified representation of an expert system involving databases and rules

In this case, an *expert system* could have human-fed knowledge about lots of different kinds of learning activities, and how they can be used together, in the form of pre-designed templates. And then for each *competency* to be met, a "rule" could be written into an algorithm to do some matchmaking between the two. Think about it as a well-maintained large flowchart made by teachers.

If you think that the example of a teacher having perfectly structured knowledge and a decision-making system in his or her head is a little far-fetched today, because the complexity of teaching in the classroom makes it so complicated to operate in such a neat mindset, try to draw your inspiration from the decision-making of a doctor, who combines bits and pieces of his or her troves of scientific knowledge to deduce a specific medical problem. Unsurprisingly, one of the earliest successes in *expert systems*—MYCIN—was designed to diagnose bacteria causing infections, and consequently recommend antibiotics.[7]

Tool to try	Business rules engines are a category of tools for large organizations to create their own *expert systems*, which uniquely solve their own process's problems. People in the domain, for example, individual subject expert teachers in our case, can write "heuristics"—simple non-mathematically perfect rules to identify or approach a problem—into the rules engines, such that when such situations arise, the rules engine can recommend or direct a workflow or solution. Drools ($$$) is a business rules engine that is free for organizations of all types and sizes to use, even though it might need your IT friend to get involved if you want to try it out.

Data hunger

FIGURE 6.2 Medium data hunger

Curriculum Development and Alignment ◆ 121

> An *expert system* tries to encapsulate and give reasoning for decisions similar to what an expert may have given when asked a query in a specific domain. Since we can guess that experts accumulate anywhere from hundreds to tens of thousands of pieces of data, an *expert system* would attempt to capture a similar amount of data points.

New vocabulary	The second way to figure out what sequence of curricular and instructional experiences will most optimally help us meet a given desired *competency* is student-driven: to build **students models** (or learner *models*).[8] *Student models* are a broad category and may have multiple meanings relating to *predicting* student brain abilities and cognitive processes. But, in this case, these are *models* that try to *predict* students' knowledge based on student responses to diagnostic probes and formative quizzes.
	Since we only see their responses to specific isolated, yet repetitive questions, but their real knowledge is hidden to us, we can use a special kind of *Hidden Markov Modeling* technique called **Bayesian Knowledge Tracing (BKT)**.[9] *BKT* updates the probability that a student knows each *competency* assessed by a question, thereby building a *model* that represents student progress and gaps in knowledge. A newer technique for *student modeling* called **Deep Knowledge Tracing** accomplishes the same goal using *deep learning* with *RNN*-based *models*.[10]
	Using *student models* made from *knowledge tracing*, AI is equipped with knowledge on what likely gaps in student proficiency in the targeted *competencies* exist for any given *competency*. This knowledge is invaluable at sequencing instruction; if one *competency*'s probability of being answered dramatically increases after another *competency* is met, that other *competency* is likely a prerequisite.

> *Tool to try* Carnegie Learning's Cognitive Tutor, a digital mathematics learning tool for students, was one of the first commercially available products that used *Knowledge Tracing* to personalize learning pathways beginning in the early 1990s, initially for Algebra.
>
> Similar products for teachers include ALEKS ($$$) (which is based on a similar idea called "Knowledge Spaces") and China's Squirrel AI Learning (Yixue).

Using a combination of *expert systems* or *student models*, it is possible to come up with the sequence in which we may target the *competencies* without creating critical gaps in understanding. They may also offer insight on differentiation opportunities for different kinds of curricular and instructional experiences.

> *New vocabulary* The most popular basis for determining which *competencies* may need to be revisited, remediated, and differentiated in *Intelligent Tutoring Systems* is **mastery learning**.[11] *Mastery learning* is an idea or strategy popularized by an educator named Benjamin Bloom,[12] who called it "Learning for Mastery" and determined that to reduce differences in students' learning progress, instructional and curricular experiences needed to be varied as much as possible to meet a students' individual learning needs. This can be diagnosed by using feedback from assessing them frequently[13] until they achieve *mastery* over those *competencies* before moving onto the next instructional unit.
>
> If the target is indeed *mastery* as described above, we can use *student models* to differentiate and sequence curriculum experiences uniquely for each student. Knowing whether or not a student will likely be able to complete the curricular experience of a certain *competency*, and having known which *competencies* they have already responded to so far, the system can begin to "adaptively" sequence one curricular experience after another. This process is sometimes called **Adaptive Content Selection**.[14]

> Alternative and often simpler techniques based on less sophisticated mathematics have had promising success. An alternative way to build *student models*, called the **Additive Factors Model**, is based on *logistic regression* (kudos if you still remember it clearly!). The general idea behind it is to *predict* how likely a student will answer a question or demonstrate success at a curricular experience based on *inputs* like "the number of times the student has had practice on that skill, the difficulty of the skill, and some general student ability." An even simpler technique, used in the site *Khan Academy*, ascertains *mastery* on a *competency* if a student answers a question correctly n-times in a row. Yep, that simple and highly effective.[15]

Tool to try	Lumilo is a wearable **real-time awareness tool** research project that shows teachers what different students in the classroom are working on, struggling with, and other *learning analytics* as they interact with the *Intelligent Tutoring Systems* in a classroom through mixed-reality smart glasses.[16] It was designed in conjunction with an *Intelligent Tutoring System* that is based on mastery learning.

But how may teachers and students access and participate in these experiences? Because these *models* may only *predict* an optimal set of guidelines like: "lecture on topic A first, and then B, and then do some guided practice using A and B together, then an application question," what about the specific activities or choices of texts along with it?

In case you are familiar with *Intelligent Tutoring Systems*, you are probably thinking that my questions are irrelevant, since we already have the materials in our hands. In such systems, exercises have often been authored by teachers or (human) curriculum developers and tied to specific *competencies*. And the goal of the system is to pick which *competency* is best suited for a student in the moment, using the previously discussed *Adaptive Content Selection* techniques.

But our goal isn't only limited to how *Intelligent Tutoring Systems* have worked in the past, so questions about specific activities or choices of texts are very valid to ask at this stage. Additionally, we have a higher benchmark: what if these activities or choices of texts don't already exist? This targets a practical limitation of inequity in curriculum access and the enormity of opportunity in curriculum quality improvement around the world. So, this will be the focus of our next and final step around making materials come to life with the help of AI.

Generating and Identifying Teachable Materials

This is the final of the three steps of the curriculum development process that we have been discussing. Materials that teachers teach with and students learn with are the lifeblood of learning. In textbook-driven learning cultures, such materials are everything. Even otherwise, they play a hugely vital role in building knowledge in a student's independent learning time, when no other support is around. They are also very difficult to create—and thus we often leave that job to big curriculum publishers. This pushes teachers out of the process very often.

Let's discuss two particular kinds of teaching materials here: what I am calling (a) **consumable knowledge**, and (b) **assessment for learning**. These two are often intentionally sequenced and intertwined with one another—for example, paragraphs of explanation in a textbook chapter followed by questions that check for understanding. But before we explore them, we need to discuss the differences between the materials made for different subjects.

Let's consider two main categories: content in the sciences & mathematics, and content in the humanities & arts. The materials in two categories are very different, even though you can sometimes find a little overlap in the means used to assess the knowledge found in both these categories.

Content in the sciences & mathematics is primarily based on facts, observations (sometimes narrative), theories, and the application of these in new contexts. For students to master content in the sciences & mathematics, they are expected to be able to reproduce these (i.e., *facts, observations, theories, and applications*) and often use a combination of them to reason or argue or deduce something not entirely spelled out.

Content in the humanities & arts, on the other hand, are based on absorbing and interpreting creative works, understanding other interpretations, and producing these works. For students to master content in the humanities & arts, they are expected to analyze, infer, and create or perform new works.

In both cases, students are often expected to memorize some theory and consequently reproduce it, before doing the more "higher-order" work.

AI gives us tools for generating content both in the sciences and the arts. I know you're thinking: "Wait, what?! AI writing educational materials and books? How could those *predictions* possibly turn into content? You're kidding!"

No, I am not! Modern AI tools can be used to generate explainer content (as seen in textbooks and articles), multiple choice, short-response, or open-ended long answer questions—often in good sequences, rubrics to assess these, practice problems, recommendations of text pairings, and more. These may be vetted and enriched with human oversight and intervention before becoming ready-to-teach plans.

Consumable Knowledge

Let's start off with discussing *consumable knowledge*. *Consumable knowledge* comes in many forms. Sciences & mathematics are usually explained through descriptive text with diagrams, pictures, charts, formulae, and derivations. A narrative form of these can be represented in multimedia forms like video.

Such text, diagrams, charts, and derivations are constructed from facts, observations, theories, and applications primarily found in dense summarizations of even more voluminous research and evidence published in journals and books. Primary sources are rarely referred to in production of K–12 learning materials around the world.

So, essentially, most of the human effort going into making knowledge consumable for students comes from humans taking existing summarizations and further summarizing or massaging them.

New vocabulary	Can we find a way for machines to *predict* the best summaries, so that humans don't have to do all the heavy lifting?
	Discourse is a sub-domain of study within *NLP* dedicated to teaching machines to understand the relationships between sentences to produce text like humans. Specifically, a topic area called automatic text summarization, or often just **summarization**,[17] is focused on using *machine learning* techniques, and increasingly *deep learning*, to perform this same task.
	The big idea: give a *model* a bulk of text—could be as big as an entire chapter—as *input*, and it will give you a *predicted* summary at a granularity of your liking. Such *pattern recognition*, if you remember from a much earlier discussion, can be accomplished by building a *model* based on *supervised learning*, one of the two types of *machine learning*. As a quick refresher, *supervised learning* is when you have examples of *inputs* and then the resulting *prediction output*, to *train* the *model*. In this case, you'd have to start off with examples of long pieces of unsummarized text, along with matching human summaries.
	When we talk about *predicting* a summary, note that we are not necessarily talking about "Cliff notes" here; textbooks are usually a summary themselves, at a high-level of granularity.
	While the statistical techniques to do *summarization* vary and are constantly undergoing iteration and rethinking, they often find themselves in one of two buckets: **extraction** or **abstraction**.[18] Techniques in these buckets are exactly what they sound like, but let's spell them out.

Extraction techniques focus on *predicting* the most important parts of the unsummarized piece of content, often anchored by key sentences with critical new information. Eventually, these are stitched together.

In this case, we are referring to *extraction* from one single piece of text, like a chapter. But nothing stops us from doing this with multiple pieces of text from different sources on the same topic. Before we do that, though, it would be useful to uncover a broader understanding from across these **pieces of text**. One technique that understands the connection between different **pieces of text** is **topic modeling**. *Topic modeling*, done through *unsupervised learning* methods involving the use of probability,[19] helps us understand the implicit groupings of information and topics in these different pieces of text.

The alternative approach to do *summarization* is *abstraction*. *Abstraction* tries to build a more complex understanding of the meaning conveyed by a text: *What are the key entities (often people or things or places, etc.) involved? How are they related? How do they change? What do they really mean?*

The people who work on improving *abstraction* aim to shine at answering such questions through the summary the model creates.

Just to make things even clearer, here is an example to show the difference between *summarization* and *abstraction*. A *summarization* of the popular fable "The Three Little Pigs" would probably begin with "Once upon a time there was an old sow with three little pigs. She sent them out to seek their fortune. Presently came along a wolf, and knocked at the door" and so on. Here, you can see that both the story and key phrases and sentences are intact. On the other hand, an *abstraction* might begin with "A mother sent her three pig children to build houses. The first built a house of straw. A wolf blew it down and ate him." Here the meaning is intact, but the language has changed.

When humans summarize larger pieces of text, we do something similar. Sometimes we build a more complex understanding and try to simplify it in our own words. Other times, we just quote the most important pieces of original texts that give us what we want.

> *New vocabulary*
>
> But what does this complex understanding built through *abstraction* look like?
>
> It looks like the *knowledge graph representation* that we have discussed previously when discussing *KRR*. The connected bubbles kind that we saw in an earlier chapter. More specifically, in *NLP*, one recent popular kind of these *representations* is called **Abstract Meaning Representation** (AMR),[20] a kind of "treebank." Just like how everyone has a unique style of taking handwritten notes with self-invented symbols, lines, and abbreviations, so that they can quickly grasp the ideas when studying them, computers also need their own semantic structure (or "meaning representation") to capture the complexity and store natural language, so that they can do calculations or analysis on them. Here is how a computer might store the sentence "the cat likes to hunt" in *AMR*:
>
>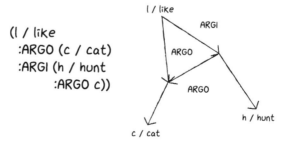
>
> **FIGURE 6.3** An Abstract Meaning Representation example with the graph form on the right-hand side
>
> Don't worry, you don't need to understand how it works and what each thing up here means.

> Why did we need yet another way to store text, though? In an earlier chapter, we discussed computers storing letters as numbers and placing them into *matrices*. But if we left all text as sequences of numbers, we could only make *predictions* of the what-follows-what or what-translates-to-what kind. Meaning representations like *AMR* allow computers to do a lot more, like constructing new sentences and phrases from such a form. This is done using techniques from *Natural Language Generation*. Among others, a set of techniques for what's called **paraphrase generation**[21] (or just paraphrasing) can be used to preserve the meaning of essential *entities*, while avoiding forcing in an out-of-context phrase from the source text. Unlike *summarization*, *paraphrase generation* doesn't intentionally discard information in language that doesn't seem to be of highest importance.

Tool to try	Algorithmia ($$$) is a platform of tools for software programmers to quickly use *machine learning models* that have been *trained* already. The platform has a "Summarizer API" service that summarizes a large piece of text into a desired size. You can try it out too without needing to program!

That wraps our thinking about generating *consumable knowledge* about the sciences. Now we come to the humanities & arts (including languages). In the humanities & arts, as we discussed earlier, the content is the creative work itself.

New vocabulary	Earlier in the book, we focused on *training* AI to *predict* something that is already there, like an image of student work, or sounds they produce, etc. At some point, we began discussing AI that can "synthesize" speech. This was a dramatic shift in our initial idea that AI can only take in data and tell us something about it. We now know it could also create—a paradigm that is often called **generative modeling** or **generative AI**.
	We can take this a step further. Scientists found ways to use *generative modeling* to not just alter what is known and can alternatively be created by a human, but go further and use inspiration from human work to generate creative works that are novel. This includes artwork, music, poetry, stories, and more.

> The techniques used for this are cumulatively called **Generative Adversarial Networks** (GANs).[22] They involve two *neural networks*: a **generator** and a **discriminator**. A *generator* is like a *speech synthesis model* in the way that it creates new things: sound, images, movements, sentences, etc. In creative works, these new things may or may not be any good. A *discriminator*, on the other hand, takes as *input* both new things from the *generator* AND from already well-known artwork, music, poetry, or stories, and *predicts* whether the new things seem human generated or machine generated.[23]
>
> In this process, the *generator model* gets better and better *trained* on what it should *output* so the *discriminator* will consider it realistic.

While we have seen a surge of interesting work in *machine learning* creating new narrative media like stories, poems, music, or even artwork in recent times through *generative modeling*, this doesn't have many tangible direct applications to teaching and learning today. That's unless we turn our attention to kindergarten and elementary school classrooms that really lack decent story/picture books or your middle school doesn't have a funded library with young adult fiction books, which isn't an uncommon problem in low-resourced schools around the world. At the same time, however, since access to potentially *generated* works depends on digital or print access, it creates only marginally more opportunities than just access to the already large amount of freely accessible works online.

    Instead, a problem that teachers and instructional leaders in schools often face is finding existing creative works that their students are ready for, or ones that align well with the philosophy of the school and the community it belongs to. For example, music and arts teachers in schools in a diverse community with a rich native or aboriginal community are always looking for students to learn the culture of the land within their curriculum. This is not easy to find, even when a digital library of these materials is available. That is because most repositories of such materials on the Internet usually allow simplistic ways to search for and filter these materials that work shallowly for a large number of materials: like name, file size, format, etc. More advanced repositories allow searching by other properties, like word count, reading difficulty, page count, topics, etc., but these depend on human labeling and tagging of materials, which is either inconsistent or missing very often because of the amount of work it takes on the part of the creator.

Gladly, advancements in AI have figured out how to *predict* properties of different works, whether they be text, music, or artwork. This ability to identify properties of creative works allows us to better identify works that target specific *competencies*.

In the case of texts, such properties may loosely capture rhetorical features, word frequency, sentence length, etc. This opens the door to evaluating how complex a text is without human involvement, in ways that only qualitative techniques have in the past. And consequently, it creates possibilities for doubling down on the effort to target students with texts that they should read fluently by the end of their grade-levels.

New vocabulary	Evaluating a text qualitatively is not the only dimension on which one can try to determine how complex a piece of text is.[24] A more common dimension in which researchers in literacy have historically shined is determining ways to quantitatively evaluate the complexity of a text. That is, by using mathematics to unpack the complexity of words and sentences in a piece of text.
	You have probably heard of quantitative evaluations of books like its "Lexile" level (a number from 0 to mid-1000s for each text), which, as it turns out, are some mathematical calculations used to determine what level a text is meant for. This is one of many alternatives that include ATOS, Degrees of Reading Power®, Flesch-Kincaid, Easability Indicator, etc. Most of these are based on a different formula for calculating how complex a text is. While the formulae of some of these are known publicly, others are kept a secret.

> In general, they use aspects like word frequency, sentence length, and text cohesion to make this formula[25]—things we tend to associate with possible reading difficulty for students. They have been a very widely used tool in helping teachers identify "leveled" texts for their students.

Tool to try	Accelerated Reader Bookfinder ($$$) is a fiction and non-fiction book search tool that allows teachers and students to find English and Spanish books based on their Lexile and ATOS reading levels, apart from other attributes.

What about creative works? Many creative works cannot be assigned properties based on fixed criteria, like text complexity can. One could argue that, in fact, what makes these works creative in the first place is their multi-dimensional not-easy-to-articulate nature. This is important to answer before we wrap up our discussion of the first part on consumable knowledge of step three in the curriculum development process, that is, "generating and identifying teachable materials," since our deepest understanding of the human condition, and therefore our world, comes from creative works.

Gladly, in cases of creative works, advancements in AI have figured out how to *loosely capture* properties such as genre, cohesiveness of ideas and elements, information density and demands, intelligences.[26]

New vocabulary	What techniques and areas in AI identify different properties of literary, music, or artistic works?
	Techniques to identify such properties are generally two kinds: **feature engineering** and **feature learning**.[27] While we have discussed them informally before, we can now use this new terminology to identify the kind of technique when we talk about one or the other.
	In the first kind, *feature engineering*, we try to determine the different properties across the works either manually or through some algorithm. We may come up with formula (or most likely use an existing one) that determines the extent of a certain property in a text. Many of the quantitative formulae used to determine text complexity discussed above are based on *feature engineering*.

Curriculum Development and Alignment ◆ 133

> Another example to classify the theme of a piece of text would be using a **bag-of-words** *model*. This is a simple technique wherein once common filler words (like "to," "and," "or," "the," etc.) are removed, we calculate the frequency of appearance of certain keywords. When we compare these frequencies to a table of themes mapped to common words, we can *predict* a theme.
>
> At times when there isn't an easy formula or logic to determine the property associated with different works, we use a second kind of techniques of *feature learning* (another way to say *machine learning* of *features*). We can use many of the *supervised and unsupervised learning* techniques, including things like *neural networks*, to *predict* the *features*. This would result in a *model* that, just given a creative work, *predicts* either a *class* or a *probability* of a certain property.
>
> Based on these features as *inputs*, further *clustering techniques* could be used to group works that are closely related to each other, or explore those that are distant in certain specific ways, for exposing students to drastically different things.

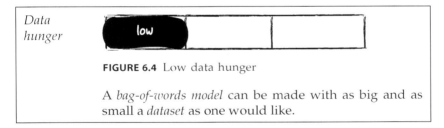

FIGURE 6.4 Low data hunger

A *bag-of-words model* can be made with as big and as small a *dataset* as one would like.

Identifying and grouping related works allows us to quickly construct sets of cohesive works to expose students to, presenting an opportunity to make huge strides in finding more personalized and differentiated materials.

Naturally, that leads us to ask: when it comes to literary and informational texts, can we treat it more like other creative works? In the *feature engineering* formulae we covered while discussing text complexity, we picked which aspects were of importance, for example, word frequency, sentence length, and text cohesion, beforehand, when calculating the single number score. Can we go beyond this single number and broad generalization to use *feature/machine learning* here as well?

New vocabulary	*Machine learning* has been the basis for new strides in better determination of general text complexity levels.
	The strides we have made primarily arise either from more advanced linguistic *features* that can be drawn from advanced *representations* of the text,[28] or from using *language models* and *deep neural networks* where the right *features* are *learned*. Having better *language models* means that we can better *predict* if words appearing in a sentence are unlikely to appear near each other, thereby indicating a possibly more uncommon lexical structure, and therefore possibly being more complex to read.

Better understanding of text complexity through *feature engineering* and *feature learning* helps us get much better at matching classrooms with texts. That said, there is still a lot of work to be done in matching individuals, and not entire classrooms, to texts,[29] especially because we know that not only are reading levels different around the world, but that every student has a different pool of vocabulary knowledge from their individual experiences and background knowledge. And that doesn't even take into account needs of second/foreign language learners.

It also does not even begin to address more fundamental problems with these formulae, for example, them "[overstating] the complexity of a piece of informational writing that uses a lot of uncommon words central to its topic" or "[understating] the complexity of a piece of narrative fiction that uses a lot of dialogue, which involves short sentences."[30]

And thus, true personalization of text complexity is still far away.

Assessment for Learning

Now let's switch our focus to *assessment for learning*. This should not be confused with assessment **of** learning, because the primary purpose of assessment of learning is to measure and not learn or teach.

Assessments for learning, in textbooks or on online learning courses, are often found in the form of questions in exercises and activities prior to, in the middle, and at the end of *consumable knowledge* explanations. In a classroom, these are usually the guided and unguided practice activities. They come in all shapes and sizes, from quick "True or False" option formative assessments to multi-lesson *performance tasks*. They have one key purpose: learn by responding/performing/applying.

In texts from both sciences and arts, students are expected to seek and respond with key pieces of textual evidence initially, but then build more complex analyses based on these facts and applications to unseen problems, situations, or settings.

In a chapter earlier in the book, we discussed modern AI's capabilities in reading written student work and listening to oral work produced by students in order to assess it. But that assumed that a teacher did a lot of the heavy lifting, including often setting out the rubric for expected answers. Also, it didn't seem like the answers had a lot of room for flexibility or creativity on a student's part. Let's go one step further in exploring what mix of techniques AI gives us to both generate questions, answer keys, and consequently check student answers.

New vocabulary	When it comes to responding to questions based on texts, techniques in AI—particularly in *NLP*—that do this fall under the problem area of **reading comprehension**,[31] which is exactly what we call it when humans do the same task.
	As I discussed before, *question answering* systems' *question generators* can engage in generating questions and picking out pieces of the response to evaluate their correctness. When used on *consumable knowledge* like in textbooks, they build questions based on the *graph representations* talked about above.

> Simple questions—basic *who*, *what*, and even *why* questions—can easily be *generated* based on the relationship between any two "nodes" (the circles) on the *graph*, especially if these *graphs* hold lots of meaning in the relationships between these nodes. These questions don't have to seek responses limited to phrases or sentences near them; often the same people or things (*entities*) are referred to in multiple ways across a piece of text, and students should be expected to make connections. The set of techniques for machines to identify multiple references to the same *entities*, for the purpose of consequently generating questions in our case, is called **coreference resolution**.[32]

Tool to try	Stanford Question Answering Dataset (SQuAD) Explorer ($$$) is an online tool that helps you explore how different *machine learning models* answer *reading comprehension* questions associated with a large number of Wikipedia articles. Allen Institute for AI, a nonprofit AI research institute, has built a demo ($$$) of a *model* that allows you to do the same on text you provide.

Even though basic questions like *who* and *what* seem to not require strong comprehension skills on the part of students, asking several of these questions—when asked in a focused instructional session—can set a strong foundation for students to answer more higher-order questions later.

New vocabulary	But can we do better than just producing basic questions? Setting higher-quality higher-order application-driven tasks remains a problem that isn't entirely solved. Apart from other reasons, this requires AI to build **common sense understanding** (yes, that's the technical AI term for it) and a lot of real examples of what constitute good and novel problems and scenarios—which we are woefully short of.[33]

Curriculum Development and Alignment ◆ 137

> For example, think of the sentence "A man went to a restaurant. He ordered a sandwich. He left a big tip." Most commonly available AI *models* today would not be able to summarize or paraphrase this action as one of "eating," because that word wasn't spoken anywhere.[34] Now, imagine the large number of ways we could have said those same sentences, and still run into the same problem, and the number of problems we can run into with other explicitly unwritten things about the man going to the restaurant for food. Now imagine all the things that could ever be said about anything, and the number of things that need to be known that did not get communicated explicitly in the text.
>
> One of the other reasons we are short of real examples is because we need to understand the progression of human thought and the sequence of building up understanding, which might be different from a machine-learned optimal pathway. And it is extremely difficult to *label datasets* to support all this knowledge.
>
> A topic area of *NLP* that is still in its infancy but making admirable progress in one aspect of building a more complex understanding of the text is called **argument mining**. It is defined as "automated detection of the argumentation structure and classification of both its component elements and their argumentative relationships."[35] In essence, techniques in this space can help us access pieces of arguments in an informational or argumentative text in an automated way, and consequently question students on relationships between pieces like, for example, the counterargument and the conclusion.

Good tasks come with clear rubrics for guiding and evaluating performance. Often, this is a laborious step in assessment design that assessment planners drop when it's crunch time.

But rubrics don't have to be handcrafted. With enough exemplars of a wide range of responses or performances or student products, *clustering* mechanisms tied with some of the

NLP tricks explained above can help build buckets of responses along different categories or dimensions, which can be used by both teacher and computer evaluators. Through this process, a teacher may be able to identify the most important "look-fors" in grading student work, and also examples of different levels and kinds of performance for each "look-for."

One of the advantages of using *question generators* based on texts is that they do not stray away from the text and require students to make evidence-based claims. This has been found to be an extremely effective literacy strategy,[36] which is in contrast with questioning about disconnected worldly conversations that do less to engage students and more to reduce the value to deeper focus on texts.

With a desire to make refinement across the three steps of the entire curriculum development and alignment process—(1) understanding of content or knowledge in the domain, (2) determining how to meet learning outcomes, and (3) generating and identifying teachable materials—one can't help but believe that AI is not very far from playing a more crucial role in a process that we believed to be extremely high-skill human-capital intensive.

| *New classrooms* | Ms. Wuku uses national standards to teach a couple of subjects. She also uses state or province learning outcome statements for another couple of subjects, and learning objectives written within the school for the rest of the subjects. In the past, all of these sets of statements were kept and maintained in different binders that were catching dust. |

Now, they have an online tool to list all of these as competencies. More so, the school has adopted a practice to link all pieces of curriculum, planning, and assessment to these competencies on the same tool. This allows Ms. Wuku to see a dashboard on which she can pull up any student's information on a laptop on parent–teacher conference day. This dashboard tracks the student against assessment performance on all these competencies and automatically generates a printable summary of the pieces of content that the student needs to revisit from their textbook and supplementary resources to get up to speed with the rest of the class, instead of her leaving the parents only with "he/she needs to work harder."

In Ms. Wuku's school, students of various backgrounds and abilities study, as it is a school that is required to accept all students to promote universal access to education. And thus, to fulfill the equal opportunity policy, there was a tendency to treat every student the same. According to them, if one student can learn, every student can learn. Students who did not show progress in learning were met with harsh words. Every teacher differed in his/her actions, and this led to a tense relationship among the academic staff.

But today, things look different because the school doesn't just recognize that every student is different; it also has a more nuanced mechanism to identify learning challenges and resolve them. This nuanced mechanism is a mobile app that lets Ms. Wuku enter what she is teaching, a little information on the student struggling, and what learning challenge she observes the student is facing. Then, based on a series of questions, the app shows suggested interventions, remedies, and differentiation ideas. Ms. Wuku can try these interventions, remedies, and differentiation ideas out, and go back and report findings from a menu of multiple selectable choices and be led further to more specific solutions. The school has integrated information on how they reorganize learning based on conclusions the app reports, and this information eventually allows Ms. Wuku to recommend a pathway to the student and his/her parents.

Ms. Wuku's school offers remedial tutoring after school hours for students struggling to keep pace with their peers. Teachers get to spend an hour with 4–7 students in every tutoring session. So far, in every session, Ms. Wuku went over the same material she covered in class earlier in the day all over again, but slowly. This was not just exhausting for Ms. Wuku, but also involved a lot of repetitive instruction.

Now, she is able to reduce the tutoring hours by half because of the support of their new online tool that links to the competencies, assessments, and curriculum. This new tool lets her print a custom exercise sheet for every student she is tutoring. Now, most of the tutoring session time is spent on students doing independent work on these sheets. At the end of the session, she collects the sheets, grades them, and enters the results into the online tool. The online tool determines exactly where each student is in his/her learning trajectory, and generates two things: (a) competencies and content that Ms. Wuku should re-teach in the next session either individually or to everyone, and (b) new personalized exercise sheets for the next tutoring session.

Early in her teaching career, Ms. Wuku realized that for students to relate to political events in the last century, it is vital for them to read history and civics not just as a series of facts, but also as personal accounts of people involved in shaping this history and civics. Whether it be accounts by change-makers in Latin America, Asia, Africa, or Europe, every time she teaches a unit on a different region, she becomes keen to take a deep dive into the writing describing the leaders, through biographies and autobiographies. She used to often look for that right chapter, speech, or anecdote that teaches students a theme, and not just facts. This took her weeks of reading in the past, in preparation.

Preparation time looks a lot different for her now, after she installed a new browser extension her friends told her about. On her favorite digital library which the

> school buys her a subscription to, she clicks on the button "Summarize chapters" on each of the books of interest to her. Within a few minutes, she can see 200-word summaries to each book. A book selection process that used to take her months now takes her a few hours.
>
> Sometimes, Ms. Wuku asks students to do independent research and bring civics articles from home from current events found in magazines, newspapers, and, for those who have access to the Internet, online sources. She asks students to read the articles carefully and present a summary of their reading to the whole class. In the past, she sat and listened like other students as the speaking student summarized it in front of the class, but she was never sure if the student ever read the whole text they were presenting to the class or just read a summary in the first paragraph or so. She never had the time to read through 32 articles between the start of the class and time for student presentations.
>
> Now, she is on top of things. She asks students to turn in the articles in print first thing in the morning. Using her high-speed scanner, she is able to have all the pages scanned and turned into words and sentences. And then she uploads all the articles to a new web-based tool where all these articles are analyzed and a set of ten comprehension questions is generated for each article. When Ms. Wuku clicks on the question, the portion of the text which has the answer gets highlighted, and the tool's expected answer to the question is shown on the side. Since she has started using this tool in class on read-and-share days, no student has been able to slip past without having closely read the text.

Notes

1. Wikipedia: Errors in the *Encyclopædia Britannica* that have been corrected in Wikipedia. (2021). In *Wikipedia*. Retrieved from https://en.wikipedia.org/w/index.php?title=Wikipedia:Errors_in_the_Encyclop%C3%A6dia_Britannica_that_have_been_corrected_in_Wikipedia&oldid=1002304806.

2 Banko, M., & Etzioni, O. (2007). Strategies for lifelong knowledge extraction from the web. *Proceedings of the 4th International Conference on Knowledge Capture*, 95–102. Retrieved from https://doi.org/10.1145/1298406.1298425.

3 Brachman, R., Pagnucco, M., & Levesque, H. (2004). *Knowledge representation and reasoning*. Germany: Elsevier Science.

4 Navigli, R., & Ponzetto, S. P. (2012). BabelNet: The automatic construction, evaluation and application of a wide-coverage multilingual semantic network. *Artificial Intelligence*, 193, 217–250.

5 Koedinger, K. R., Corbett, A. T., & Perfetti, C. (2012). The Knowledge-Learning-Instruction framework: Bridging the science–practice chasm to enhance robust student learning. *Cognitive Science*, 36(5), 757–798.

6 Engelmore, R. S. (1987). Artificial intelligence and knowledge based systems: Origins, methods and opportunities for NDE. In D. O. Thompson & D. E. Chimenti (Eds.), *Review of progress in quantitative nondestructive evaluation*. Boston, MA: Springer, 1–20.

7 Engelmore (1987).

8 Chrysafiadi, K., & Virvou, M. (2013). Student modeling approaches: A literature review for the last decade. *Expert Systems with Applications*, 40(11), 4715–4729.

9 Corbett, A. T., & Anderson, J. R. (1994). Knowledge tracing: Modeling the acquisition of procedural knowledge. *User modeling and user-adapted interaction*, 4(4), 253–278.

10 Piech, C., Bassen, J., Huang, J., Ganguli, S., Sahami, M., Guibas, L., & Sohl-Dickstein, J. (2015). Deep knowledge tracing. *Proceedings of the 28th International Conference on Neural Information Processing Systems—Volume 1*, 505–513.

11 Block, J. H., & Burns, R. B. (1976). Mastery learning. *Review of Research in Education*, 4, 3–49.

12 Bloom, B. S. (1968). Learning for mastery. *Evaluation Comment* (UCLA-CSIEP), 1(2), 1–12.

13 Guskey, T. R. (2007). Closing achievement gaps: Revisiting Benjamin S. Bloom's "Learning for mastery." *Journal of Advanced Academics*, 19(1), 8–31.

14 Doroudi, S. (2017). *Computation, Constructivism, and Curriculum Design*.

15 Pelánek, R., & Řihák, J. (2017). Experimental analysis of mastery learning criteria. *Proceedings of the 25th Conference on User Modeling, Adaptation and Personalization*, 156–163. Retrieved from https://doi.org/10.1145/3079628.3079667.
16 Holstein, K., McLaren, B. M., & Aleven, V. (2018). Student learning benefits of a mixed-reality teacher awareness tool in AI-enhanced classrooms. In C. Penstein Rosé, R. Martínez-Maldonado, H. U. Hoppe, R. Luckin, M. Mavrikis, K. Porayska-Pomsta, B. McLaren, & B. du Boulay (Eds.), *Artificial intelligence in education*. New York: Springer International Publishing, 154–168.
17 Nenkova, A., & McKeown, K. (2012). A survey of text summarization techniques. In *Mining Text Data*. Boston, MA: Springer, 43–76.
18 Allahyari, M., Pouriyeh, S., Assefi, M., Safaei, S., Trippe, E. D., Gutierrez, J. B., & Kochut, K. (2017). A brief survey of text mining: Classification, clustering and extraction techniques. *ArXiv:1707.02919* [Cs]. Retrieved from http://arxiv.org/abs/1707.02919.
19 Liu, L., Tang, L., Dong, W., Yao, S., & Zhou, W. (2016). An overview of topic modeling and its current applications in bioinformatics. *SpringerPlus*, 5(1), 1608.
20 Banarescu, L., Bonial, C., Cai, S., Georgescu, M., Griffitt, K., Hermjakob, U., ... & Schneider, N. (2013, August). Abstract meaning representation for sembanking. In *Proceedings of the 7th Linguistic Annotation Workshop and Interoperability with Discourse* (pp. 178–186).
21 Barzilay, R., & Lee, L. (2003). Learning to paraphrase: An unsupervised approach using multiple-sequence alignment. *Proceedings of the 2003 Human Language Technology Conference of the North American Chapter of the Association for Computational Linguistics* (pp. 16–23). www.aclweb.org/anthology/N03-1003
22 Goodfellow, I., Pouget-Abadie, J., Mirza, M., Xu, B., Warde-Farley, D., Ozair, S., Courville, A., & Bengio, Y. (2014). Generative adversarial nets. In *Advances in Neural Information Processing Systems*. New York: Curran Associates, Inc.
23 Generative Artificial Intelligence (n.d.). Retrieved February 23, 2018 from www.youtube.com/watch?v=PhCM3qoRZHE.

24 Pearson, P. D., & Hiebert, E. H. (2013). *The state of the field: Qualitative analyses of text complexity* (Reading Research Report 13.01). TextProject, Inc.
25 *Supplemental Information for Appendix A of the Common Core State Standards for English Language Arts and Literacy: New Research on Text Complexity*. (2019). Council of Chief State School Officers, National Governors Association. Retrieved from www.corestandards.org/wp-content/uploads/Appendix-A-New-Research-on-Text-Complexity-revised.pdf.
26 As in "multiple intelligences."
27 Ng, A. (n.d.). What is machine learning? *Coursera*. Retrieved from www.coursera.org/lecture/machine-learning/what-is-machine-learning-Ujm7v.
28 Kotani, K., Yoshimi, T., & Isahara, H. (2011). *A machine learning approach to measurement of text readability for EFL learners using various linguistic features*. Retrieved from https://eric.ed.gov/?id=ED529383.
29 Goldman, S. R., & Lee, C. D. (2014). Text complexity: State of the art and the conundrums it raises. *The Elementary School Journal*, 115(2), 290–300.
30 Robert, R. (2012). *The Complex Matter of Text Complexity*. Harvard Education Letter, Harvard Graduate School of Education. Retrieved from www.hepg.org/hel-home/issues/28_5/helarticle/the-complex-matter-of-text-complexity_544.
31 Rajpurkar, P., Zhang, J., Lopyrev, K., & Liang, P. (2016, November). SQuAD: 100,000+ questions for machine comprehension of text. In *Proceedings of the 2016 Conference on Empirical Methods in Natural Language Processing* (pp. 2383–2392).
32 Ng, V. (2010, July). Supervised noun phrase coreference research: The first fifteen years. In *Proceedings of the 48th Annual Meeting of the Association for Computational Linguistics* (pp. 1396–1411).
33 How to teach artificial intelligence some common sense (n.d.). *Wired*. Retrieved May 24, 2021 from www.wired.com/story/how-to-teach-artificial-intelligence-common-sense/.

34 Pavlus, J. (2020). Common sense comes to computers. *Quanta Magazine*, April 30. Retrieved February 26, 2021 from www.quantamagazine.org/common-sense-comes-to-computers-20200430/.
35 Moens, M.-F. (2018). Argumentation mining: How can a machine acquire common sense and world knowledge? *Argument & Computation*, 9(1), 1–14.
36 *Common Core State Standards for English Language Arts & Literacy in History/Social Studies, Science, and Technical Subjects Appendix A*. (2010). Common Core State Standards Initiative. Retrieved from www.corestandards.org/assets/Appendix_A.pdf.

7

Deeper, Higher-order, Authentic Learning

Every now and then, thanks to the merit of hardworking teachers and administrators, schools are able to get the basics right: low achievement disparities, no kid going hungry, functioning infrastructure, support for students with needs, a solid curriculum, and satisfied teachers.

It is at these times that educators, and mostly education researchers, advocates, and champions, begin to wonder: can students be learning more than the bare minimum? … learning for immersion and fascination with topics? … learning for solving real-world problems? … learning for accomplishing bigger dreams?

And, at such a moment, we begin to suggest that the answer lies in going "deeper" and doing tasks that are "higher order" on a hierarchy of cognitive difficulty or more "authentic."[1] Different educators explain these ideas differently in their contexts, but they all generally point to the same core idea, the idea of

DOI: 10.4324/9781003183235-7

making students creative, innovative, and versatile complex problem-solvers.

| New vocabulary | "Deeper Learning" and the *deep learning* we have been talking about have pretty much nothing to do with each other.[2] |

If creating learning experiences, which were deeper, higher order, and authentic, had a clear formula, or something most teachers were trained at doing very well, then this wouldn't be a problem to worry about. But as you may have guessed by the inclusion of this discussion in the book, it's not the case.

And as we digest AI's abilities in creating new learning experiences, from the last chapter, a big worry begins to question our faith in AI's ability to do a good job at it.

And That Is One of Shallowness

It is a worry where we ask: "sure AI can put together sentences that seem coherent, questioning the learner to respond with some factoids, perhaps even come up with options to confuse them—but can AI require students to dig deeper or perform more complex real-world-ish thinking engaging their highest-orders of cognitive skills?"

This turns out to be a surprisingly important question. That's because AI advancements are most useful if they move us forward, rather than magnifying our current inabilities. And the one thing we should be most careful to not magnify is our limited inability to come up with learning experiences that are not shallow or rote-learning/drill based. Such shallow or rote-learning/drill-based learning experiences are ineffective, yet very widely present today.

To be able to create such learning experiences (tasks, quizzes, lecture progressions, etc.), AI needs to first be able to evaluate whether a learning experience is deep or shallow.

New vocabulary

Coincidentally, *deep learning* may be appropriate for *predicting* how shallow a learning experience is. That may be possible if we can *train* a *model* on a fairly large number of existing good or bad exemplar learning experiences.

If we were to approach this as a *supervised learning* problem, these large numbers of learning experiences could be *labeled* by curriculum developers. To do this, we may assign a level from **Bloom's taxonomy**[3] to each learning experience. And then, a *neural network* could be designed to make high-quality *predictions* of the cognitive depth of any new learning experience a teacher or another AI designs.

If you haven't heard of *Bloom's taxonomy* before, here is a brief introduction on it: in the 1950s, an educator named Benjamin Bloom (yes, the same one who came up with *mastery learning*) collected all kinds of tasks a human mind can do while it learns. Then, he and his colleagues grouped them in a few categories by depth, thereby being called a **taxonomy**—similar to how, when we group plant or animal species, they fall under *taxonomies*. In recent times, the "revised" 2001 version[4] has been used, as shown below.

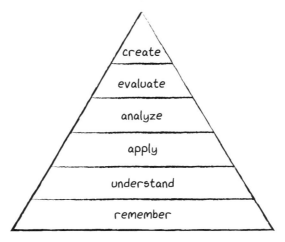

FIGURE 7.1 Revised Bloom's taxonomy

> In this pyramid, you see tiers that describe the simplest human learning tasks at the bottom. As we go up the pyramid, the tasks described by the tier increase in cognitive difficulty, and therefore depth of learning. Any learning expectations a teacher sets for a student fall somewhere along this pyramid.
>
> As suggested before, the tiers from this *taxonomy* pyramid can be used as *labels* on several students' exemplar learning experiences to build a *supervised learning model*.

In a lot of advancements in AI that we have discussed so far, particularly in sections talking about *supervised learning* techniques, a lot of the data used to make *predictions* has been *labeled* by humans.

However, in an earlier chapter on behavior management, we began to realize that just being able to have enough people *label* such data doesn't solve the problem. Such as in the problem of *speech emotion recognition*, where we discovered that human subjectivity in *labeling* data causes the AI to not work well. Such subjectivity continues in evaluating how deep a learning experience is.

New vocabulary	Human *labeling* by curriculum developers is not the only way to express how deep a learning experience is, though.
	Since most learning experiences, or at least their instructions, can be phrased and represented in a textual form like sentences, we may borrow some techniques from *NLP* and *information retrieval* to tell us some key aspects of each learning experience. Let's look at a trivialized example of an area of study called **topic discovery**—which essentially boils down to trying to deduce commonalities among a collection of things.[5] In this case, the commonality we are looking for is depth.

We can use something straightforward called **Term Frequency-Inverse Document Frequency** (TF-IDF),[6] commonly used in search engines to find the things that most reflect the words or phrases, called **n-grams**, that we are searching for. We use *n-grams* instead of "words" or "phrases" because *n-gram* can mean a phrase of any ("n") number of words.

It is a simple algorithm: for every "document," in our case for every learning experience for students to go through, we can first find the most common *n-grams* present in the task presented to students. And then, we go through every document, to see how often that *n-gram* shows up. The more it shows up across many documents, the lesser a single document's importance becomes. For example, the word "practice" or "read" repeats in almost every task. So, these two words are probably poor determinants of what the primary purpose of the learning experience is.

As a result, after running this simple algorithm on all the documents, we get a mapping between *n-grams* and the most important documents they lead to.

How does this help us identify depth of learning experiences, though? Instead of mapping just any miscellaneous *n-grams* to tasks, we can focus just on verbs. So, we get something like this, with the order of tasks reflecting relevance:

show: task 4, task 10, task 3, task 9
give example: task 2, task 1, task 9, task 10
compute: task 7, task 6, task 1, task 8
discuss: task 5, task 2, task 3, task 6
...

Interestingly, every group of *Bloom's taxonomy*, something we just discussed as a good indicator of depth of a learning experience, can be mapped to several verbs. Teachers frequently use these charts to come up with higher-order learning objectives. For example, the verb "show" falls under the "application" group of *Bloom's taxonomy*, according to one interpretation. Therefore, since these verbs serve as good proxies for the depth of learning experience, we can roughly *predict* the *Bloom's taxonomy* category each task falls in.

> If that doesn't work, *clustering* techniques from *unsupervised learning* might be able to *predict* in what "cluster" or bucket a given learning experience falls—just the way we discussed discovering properties on texts with the help of *NLP*.

| Data hunger | 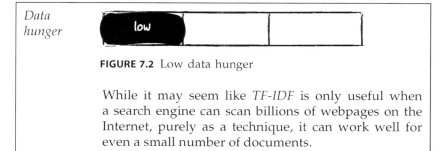 |

FIGURE 7.2 Low data hunger

> While it may seem like *TF-IDF* is only useful when a search engine can scan billions of webpages on the Internet, purely as a technique, it can work well for even a small number of documents.

Another challenge for AI in constructing learning experiences is that, in practice, we have only tried a limited set of examples of possibilities for questions/problems and the kinds of work students will produce for them, from our experience teaching them. There are plenty more permutations and combinations of questions/problems and student work we would like our *models* to learn from, beyond whatever our colleagues and our students have been introduced to.

| New vocabulary | We briefly touched upon the idea of *generative modeling* for coming up with new creative works, in the last chapter. One of its greatest strengths is in its promise to try out millions of new creations that haven't existed and *predict* how good they are without ever having to exhaust human time. |
| | Additionally, often, our data for *training models* that evaluate depth of student work is limited to finite examples of mastery or expert performance. This doesn't allow us to make a high-quality *model*. Making a *model* based on just finite examples of mastery is like asking the teacher down the corridor, who only teaches the gifted students, to tell us how teaching and learning works—what would she know about teaching students who struggle or students who don't accurately reproduce solutions, amiright? |

> *Generative modeling* opens the door to letting the computer imagine a wild number of possibilities of thinking and situations based on a wide gamut of criteria.

This allows us to use AI to magnify what we already know about support in the deeper learning process: that the best teachers often intervene with good feedback when they have seen enough novice performance,[7] variability in student work, and/or understand the depths and breadths of the subject they teach.[8]

Once we have a way to know how deep a learning experience is, AI can use that *model* or rubric or algorithm to assess whether or not a new learning experience being designed is going to turn out to be deep or not. And if it can assess this, it can try to do less of what doesn't work and more of what does. Thus, this mechanism allows us to make higher quality *models*.

Deeper Learning Experiences Over a Longer Period

Putting together everything we have discussed so far: we know, in theory, that AI can create new learning experiences. From our discussion in the last chapter, we know that gathering data on whether a student has completed specific curricular experiences that satisfy corresponding individual *competencies* allows us to adaptively create a sequence. We also know that AI could assess whether a learning experience is deep or not.

But can AI make complex, non-granular learning experiences that maximize the student's ability to transfer learning and achieve a larger goal over a series of steps, such as in the case of project-based learning? Something that gives us a holistic understanding of what sort of long-term learning pathway to build for the student?

To put it in different words, the question we are asking here is: making one-off *predictions* is well and good, but what about making *predictions* for longer-term, deeper, higher-order, authentic learning over an entire unit or an entire course? It feels like we would need to make many, many *predictions* that all play well with each other and towards a long-term goal.

| *New vocabulary* | We earlier discussed something called *Markov models* and *hidden Markov models*. These were about making *predictions* based on some prior information. This is useful to bring back because when trying to *predict* depth of learning for an entire course, we could use some thinking around decisions based on previous states and events.

So, let's talk about another "Markovian" idea called a **Markov Decision Process** (MDP). In its simplest sense, an MDP describes:

1. An **environment**—a world in which we want to study or apply *machine learning*. In our case, our world is all of our learning experiences we might create for the student.
2. It can be in different **states**—think of *states* as different points of progress or detours that someone ends up in while trying to solve a task.
3. Every step taken is an **action**. Taking an *action* changes the *state*.
4. And that someone or something that performs an *action* is an **agent**. Not the Bond kind!
5. The thinking the *agent* uses to take an *action* to result in a new *state* is called a **policy**. To remember it, think of it as analogous to *policies* politicians write that change the state of our world.
6. An *agent* taking an *action* using a *policy* receives a **reward**. This *reward* could either be positive or negative. This *reward* results in a modification of the *policy* so that the best *policy* is one whose actions generate the most *reward*. |

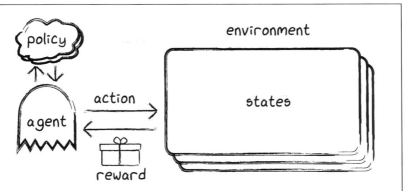

FIGURE 7.3 A Markov Decision Process visualized

You don't need to overthink this to try to look for complexity. It is simple and gives us some terminology to proceed.

Reinforcement Learning (RL) is a sub-field of *machine learning* in which *agents* try to *maximize* a sum of long-term *rewards* through the *actions* they take in the *environment*.[9]

"*Maximize* a sum of long-term *rewards*" is a mouthful. Let's unpack that a little bit with an example. Let's say our *environment* is a game of scrabble, the *agent* is a player, a *state* is any configuration of the scrabble board, and the *reward* is points you get every time the player creates a new word. A "sum of long-term *rewards*" basically means the total points made in the scrabble game. To "*maximize*" it means using mathematical ways to make sure that player gets so many points that her opponent goes home weeping.

Applying this same thinking to learning experiences, we can say our *environment* is the course being taught, an *agent* is a computerized student, and the *reward* is a deep learning experience. And that our goal is to create the deepest learning experiences for the student.

> While RL is not a new sub-field, and it has shown a lot of promise in finding *rewards* in the long term through learning from the *environment*, it works well only in problems with well-defined scopes.[10] Particularly, when it comes to sequencing instruction, it has primarily found success when programmed with clear guidelines on how the brain works and learns.[11] There is still a while to go before RL can work well in very open-ended problems like depth of learning experiences, in a way that the computer doesn't need to be told everything about the student's world and abilities and how humans learn from before. Such challenges are discussed in Chapter 9, "Challenges" later in the book.

Predicting whether a series of learning experiences is going to yield a very deep course is a very powerful idea, because it takes a huge amount of content knowledge and experience for a teacher or a curriculum developer in any domain to be able to build a little bit of this kind of understanding.

That said, it seems like our assumption here was that some *model* that *predicts* the full course depth is already known and is going to work for every course and subject. We can already guess that this is not straightforward.

New vocabulary	One spin on doing RL is called **model-free** *reinforcement learning*; in this, we don't have such a *model* in the first place. In this approach, in the case of our scenario, the full depth of the course is evaluated along the way as we offer one learning experience after another, and the system learns what works and what doesn't (the *policies*) along the way.

Also, another question comes up: is this going to create learning experiences that are all extremely deep? Are the students only going to be asked and shown very tough complex problems and nothing simple? This wouldn't be the best contender because it would make it very stressful for students.

New vocabulary	*Reinforcement Learning* is different from other kinds of *machine learning* areas because it is always focused on accomplishing the goal over a long term. Just like within a multi-step problem-based learning activity, while each step a student takes by itself might be pretty simple, at the end of the activity, the learning turns out to be deep. *RL* is just like that, and the long term in our ongoing example is the whole course. If the *policies* for taking *actions* are *learned* based on actual cognitive understanding of human ability to absorb material and make connections, each individual learning experience will reflect the best learning step for a student at that point. This understanding needs to either be based on data, or on a *student model* that more holistically reflects a student's cognitive tempo for learning. The system shouldn't be under any pressure to make each learning experience deep. Sometimes, however, when this data is less, or *states* and *actions* are complex, it is hard for AI to determine the best *policies* themselves. Additionally, the end doesn't always justify the means; just because an *action* changes the *state* to a desired one does not always mean it is the correct *action*. For example, imagine that a step of a science experiment is to mix two chemicals to create a reaction that produces heat. Now if the student merely puts the existing solution above a burner to heat it, even though the end result is what he or she expected, the step wasn't correct. In such scenarios, generally in *machine learning*, we want an expert to be constantly telling the machine along the way whether it is learning correctly. Such techniques are usually called **Human-In-The-Loop** (HITL) techniques.[12] *RL* can also be combined with *HITL* techniques to come up with the most optimal *policies*.

Tool to try	Amazon Mechanical Turk ($$$) allows anyone building AI to tap into human knowledge and judgment with a variety of skills from around the world at any time for a small cost. For example, a textbook company might use Mechanical Turk to identify all the places in their textbook where a table or image does not show on the same page as the text that describes it. Figure Eight ($$$) is another example tool that taps into a large pool of humans, specifically for *machine learning* tasks. Neither of these tools focus on teaching or content expertise, but they are examples of what is possible.
Data hunger	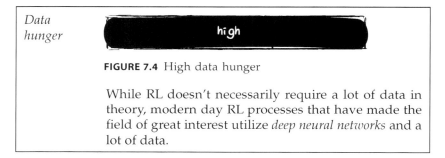 **FIGURE 7.4** High data hunger While RL doesn't necessarily require a lot of data in theory, modern day RL processes that have made the field of great interest utilize *deep neural networks* and a lot of data.

To further double down on this concern, note that a progression of learning experiences created by such an AI isn't any good if students can't reasonably engage with those experiences for long enough to productively struggle for a while to actually learn. Deep tasks that require students to keep solving problems in circles, or feel fakely concocted, will disengage students all too soon.

And so, we can push our learning-experiences-generating AI to learn the key ideas of engagement and begin to incorporate them. Engagement in the classroom begins with hooking the students through their interests, and then supporting them through the learning journey. The core dimensions of engagement, according to Stanford's Center for Opportunity Policy in Education, are[13]: **relevance, autonomy, collaboration**, and **authenticity**. That means that for a learning experience to be engaging, it may incorporate a mix of these elements.

New vocabulary	Let us consider ways in which the AI might incorporate these core aspects of engagement.

Relevance
The amazingly simple way for AI to *predict* which exercise, text, or multimedia is relevant and interesting to a group of students is by using data on what else they or another student group in similar situations found interesting. Sounds familiar? Yes, these are the same *unsupervised learning* techniques used in online shopping and video streaming apps to recommend things. They are called **recommender systems**,[14] and more specifically with what I am talking about, **collaborative filtering**. In these techniques, a *prediction* of a user's likeliness of finding a piece of learning material engaging is dependent on the rating or other engagement metric given by another user who has given similar ratings on similar learning materials.

For example, if teachers across a school district asked students to pick which Shakespeare play they wanted to perform to, using the data gathered on different students and their preferences, a *model* could be made to *predict* a student's preferences based on their grade, school, other subjects, etc.

We can also use *affect detection* to gauge student interest, as often human faces and speech are expressive when their interests are unusually peaked or tanked.

Autonomy
Learning experiences which have multiple entry points or pathways to completion, or ones that offer students the options to choose from different kinds of final products to produce, allow students with varying learning needs the autonomy to own their learning process so that they don't feel restricted by regimented bounds. So, hypothetically, a *model* that *generates* a learning experience may take in as an *input* an expected student response type. So, every student might end up with a slightly different learning experience aligned with their interest. |

For example, one student might be interested in coming up with painting a human portrait, while another might be interested in painting an animal in an art unit on painting living things. The *model* may predict the steps for these different final products for each of the students.

Collaboration

An interesting spin on single-agent *RL*, which is what we have been discussing thus far, is **multi-agent RL**, where cooperation of more than one *agent* can actually improve the efficiency of the AI. One of the aspects that can be baked into the way we lower *error* while training, which will be used to *train* the joint *policy* across agents, might be fair distribution of work. This will help us create learning experiences where cooperation enhances performance on the task.

For example, in a project assignment, it is common for one or two students in a group to take on the majority of the work. With a *model trained* for *multi-agent RL*, a project's requirements could split work in ways that, when the team comes together, the final output is even better.

Authenticity

Authentic learning experiences are real-seeming and non-made-up. This is slightly trickier to *train* a *model* with if the *labels* on the examples are fairly subjective; even expert teachers in-the-loop may not always agree on what seems authentic and what doesn't, without student feedback.

One of the more useful things we can do is collect some data about which real-world local events, scenarios, and states are interesting to students and tie them to the *competencies* we intend to teach. Using this data, we can design and *train* a *model* that *predicts* several noteworthy recent real-world events or scenarios for a given *competency*.

> For each situation or event tied to the *competency*, *we* could then use an *HITL* system to crowdsource the level of authenticity, that is, we could ask many randomly chosen people how authentic they think the situation or event is. And then use a threshold on the distribution to filter for a measure of certainty; this is another way of saying pick the ones that most people think seem authentic. These situations, in turn, could be used to build learning experiences around.

An Alternative Focus for AI

Since the majority of AI research is focused on answering questions and solving problems faster and better than humans, it often requires unconventional use of existing tools to come up with AI systems where we focus on making humans build their understanding for longer memory, transfer, intermediary steps mastery, and application to unseen problems, in the most optimal way. That's regardless of whether an AI or a teacher gets the last call on what the student learns, when.

> Understanding where a student is at, at any given time in their learning, and relaying this long-term perspective back to both machines and teachers allows for a powerful relationship between technology and humans where the process of decision-making is cooperative, not competitive.
>
> This falls under an alternative view of AI that puts human empowerment at its center, called **Intelligence Augmentation**.[15]

New vocabulary	It feels like the challenge of teachers guiding machines is suddenly staring us in the face because the extent to which teachers need to work with computers to create more learning opportunities for students is rapidly increasing and technologies are getting more complex. For example, making *human-in-the-loop* work well for RL is a problem we are only just beginning to grapple with.
	However, humans have had to work closely with technology for several decades now, beginning around the time people needed to interact with computer mouses and personal computers.[16] And during every evolution of technological progress, the factors that determined how people use technologies, and how human-friendly the technologies are, have been critical in building the relationship we have today. The field of study that has been at the forefront of progress in making humans successful in solving these problems is called **Human–Computer Interaction**. *Human–Computer Interaction* has largely focused on factors like user interface and experience design, organizational and human constraints and capabilities, and overcoming underlying psychological hurdles.

Because AI introduces so many new challenges for this human–computer relationship that go beyond just the computer's interaction with the user, particularly in the domains of ethics, sociology, and neuroscience, there are new cross-disciplinary institutions emerging in AI, sometimes involving people with backgrounds in *Human–Computer Interaction*. A couple of examples of such institutions are the Stanford Institute for Human-Centered Artificial Intelligence and UC Berkeley's Center for Human-Compatible Artificial Intelligence.

The work at such institutions focuses on an inclusive, human-centered, controlled, safe, understandable, and cooperative partnership with AI as it collides with and impacts different fields, while ensuring higher productivity and quality of life for all.

> *New classrooms*
>
> Ms. Wuku has a new batch of students every year. Her students get four to seven new teachers every academic year, ever since they enter Grade 1. So, historically, every teacher treated their students' minds like empty boxes that needed to learn the content of the year, with equal proficiency and prior knowledge.
>
> This year, her high school decided to do something different. Students are now expected to do culmination writing projects in English at the end of Grades 10 and 12 that are based on their writing interests over the years. To make this possible, Ms. Wuku uses an online tool which lists all her students, along with their topic of choice, and connects to the competencies being taught over the year and prior assessment data.
>
> When she clicks on the name of a student, she can see different activities she can do during the year to better prepare that student for the final culmination project. She can do the same for the whole batch of students, by clicking on the "Recommend class-wide activities" button. This generates a report, clustering different student groups with paired activities that best move students forward in the individual learning journeys.

Notes

1. Mehta, J., & Fine, S. (2015). *The why, what, where, and how of deeper learning in American secondary schools* (Students at the Center: Deeper Learning Research Series). Jobs for the Future.
2. This happens again with the phrase "online learning."
3. Bloom, B. S. (1956). *Taxonomy of educational objectives: The classification of educational goals Handbook I*. London: Longman.
4. Armstrong, P. (2010). *Bloom's Taxonomy*. Vanderbilt University Center for Teaching. Retrieved May 17, 2021 from https://cft.vanderbilt.edu/guides-sub-pages/blooms-taxonomy/.
5. Wallach, H. M. (2006, June). Topic modeling: Beyond bag-of-words. In *Proceedings of the 23rd International Conference on Machine Learning* (pp. 977–984).

6 Rajaraman, A., & Ullman, J. D. (2011). *Mining of massive datasets*. Cambridge: Cambridge University Press. Retrieved from https://doi.org/10.1017/CBO9781139058452.
7 Hattie, J., & Timperley, H. (2007). The power of feedback. *Review of Educational Research*, 77(1), 81–112.
8 Ball, D. L., Thames, M. H., & Phelps, G. (2008). Content knowledge for teaching: What makes it special. *Journal of Teacher Education*, 59(5), 389–407.
9 Sutton, R. S., & Barto, A. G. (2018). *Reinforcement learning: An introduction* (2nd edn, Preface). Cambridge, MA: The MIT Press.
10 Sutton & Barto (2018).
11 Doroudi, S., Aleven, V., & Brunskill, E. (2019). Where's the reward? A review of reinforcement learning for instructional sequencing. *International Journal of Artificial Intelligence in Education*, 29(4), 568–620. Retrieved from https://doi.org/10.1007/s40593-019-00187-x.
12 Amershi, S., Cakmak, M., Knox, W. B., & Kulesza, T. (2014). Power to the people: The role of humans in interactive machine learning. *AI Magazine*, 35(4), 105–120.
13 Taylor, C., Kokka, K., Darling-Hammond, L., Dieckman, J., Santana Pacheco, V., Sandler, S., & Bae, S. (2016). *Student engagement: A framework for on-demand performance assessment tasks*. Stanford, CA: Stanford Center for Opportunity Policy in Education.
14 Aggarwal, C. C. (2016). Neighborhood-based collaborative filtering. In C. C. Aggarwal (Ed.), *Recommender systems: The textbook*. New York: Springer International Publishing, 29–70. Retrieved from https://doi.org/10.1007/978-3-319-29659-3_2.
15 Shum, S. B., & Knight, S. (n.d.). Artificial intelligence holds great potential for both students and teachers—but only if used wisely. *The Conversation*. Retrieved September 19, 2018 from http://theconversation.com/artificial-intelligence-holds-great-potential-for-both-students-and-teachers-but-only-if-used-wisely-81024.
16 MacKenzie, I. S. (2013). Historical context. In *Human-computer interaction*. Amsterdam: Elsevier, 1–26. Retrieved from https://doi.org/10.1016/B978-0-12-405865-1.00001-7.

8

Teacher Education and Professional Development

Professional development in teaching, that is, learning about teaching on the job, is treated very differently from how it is in other professions. It is much more frequent, and aggressively mandatory—often on a teacher's own time and dime. In my opinion, two reasons for this are: (a) constantly changing jurisdiction/administration requirements, AND (b) pre-service teacher education programs failing to capture the complexity and opportunities in real-life teaching.

Constantly changing administration requirements are generally understandable.[1] The failure of pre-service teacher education programs—not so much. Either teaching is a surprisingly and uniquely complex profession, or teacher education programs are by and large not competent enough when it comes to imparting theoretical underpinnings and practical skills for dealing with a wide range of student demographics and content. Or it is possibly a combination of both.

DOI: 10.4324/9781003183235-8

So, Let's Start Off With a Focus on Pre-service Teacher Education Programs

Curriculum and instruction are deeply intrinsically linked; knowledge and skills cannot be introduced and advanced without the right instructional choices and command. A couple of chapters ago, we discussed how AI would one day be advanced enough to develop and improve curriculum for any subject. While this creates enormous value for an experienced teacher, it can all fall flat when those very activities are not setup, supported, and managed with the right instructional methods in the classroom.

Just great curriculum is not enough. At the end of the day, any human exchange of knowledge that is hugely dependent on performance and practice, like teaching, has a bottleneck of needing highly practical time in front of their real audience. Therefore, there are teacher residency programs; programs within the pursuit of an advanced education degree where teachers immerse themselves in schools to teach students, while taking college coursework. This has promoted the cause for teacher education programs to be "professionalized" and considered on par with medical programs when it comes to rigor, need for individual judgment, and application of independent knowledge and expertise.[2]

AI's goals revolve around teaching machines to think and act like humans. If machines can begin to act like humans, they most certainly can begin to emulate them as students. And if machines can begin to emulate students, we can vastly improve the teacher education process by creating more authentic teacher–student-interaction experiences, thereby increasing the teacher learning process by several magnitudes.

Beginning to emulate real-life student responses to curriculum and instruction targeted at them cannot always be dumbed down to situations of whether students answer the questions correctly. There is a lot that happens in a student's mind before an answer can be assessed—the intermediary steps of the work they do, visual reactions showing engagement, doubts they express, etc. The range of possibilities of each of these student-learning moments can be diverse and very complex. Students will often raise their hands, get distracted and talk to peers, get stuck for long periods, or cross-out wrongly produced written responses, apart from other signs. And these are all behaviors that those emulating real-life student responses may consider.

New vocabulary	Let's start off with a focus on AI checking student responses for understanding.
	The problem area dedicated to studying ways to understand and *model* the steps that did not lead to the ideal answers is called **misconception analysis**. Originally referred to as **buggy rules**[3] in the context of personalized mathematics and programming learning, the idea referred to the faulty "rules" used to go from one step to another, which could be captured and remediated through student feedback.
	When first discussed and proposed[4] an example of a bug was shown to be a student's simple procedural error in resetting a "1" carried over from a column on the right to a column on the left, after being used once, when adding two multi-digit numbers.

Over time, the victimization of students (by calling it "buggy" or a "misconception") has been strongly challenged by members of the AI community because "mis-steps" can be understood as manifestations of student knowledge from a prior problem or task that did not transfer well to this new task.[5] So, it isn't as much of a mistake, as it is an application whose context isn't relevant. And teachers understand this. Regardless, I will continue to use the terms "buggy" and "misconception" for the rest of the discussion for consistency, even though I don't endorse it.

There is more depth to answers or parts of answers than being right or wrong. Imagine planning out, in advance, all the possible areas of confusion a student could encounter on a question you will pose to them. And now imagine continuing to do this for a series of questions.

New vocabulary	If you're dedicated to getting all bases covered, it's unlikely that you will be satisfied with one simple list of *buggy rules*. You will probably end up making a big chart with lines connecting hundreds of misconceptions types to hundreds of questions.
	In practice, cataloging tens of misconceptions over millions of different kinds of *competencies* and then manually placing them in the equivalent of an Excel table that can be sorted on multiple columns is a very difficult thing for people to do. Such complexity of trying to represent massive amounts of possibilities of things, which have lots of *features* of similarity in varying degrees, that can't be represented in simple lists, is a problem faced in the natural language world too.
	Instead of treating a misconception as an isolated learning gap for every single *competency*, we can express it as something which resurfaces in different ways for different *competencies*. But how would we represent that information? You may remember *matrices* from the beginning of our discussion on *machine learning*. The answer to our question on representing misconceptions lies in single-row *matrices*, called **vectors.**
	In *machine learning*, such *vectors* can be *trained* using data, instead of manually by a human.[6] Such *vectors* are then sometimes called **embeddings**.[7] In our example of misconceptions, each misconception *embedding* might hold information on how closely it is related to a large number of *competencies* in a subject through learned *features*, without explicitly storing its connection to each *competency*.
	Let's try to think visually, limited by what we can show on printed paper. Say we pulled out a few misconceptions *embeddings*, which is just saying we pulled out a few misconceptions represented mathematically and therefore hard for humans to interpret. And say we tried to nitpick just three of the many *features* that represent all misconceptions, so that we could plot them visually like below. If they were two *features*, it would be a 2-D graph with an x-axis and a y-axis. Because we have a third *feature*, we add another dimension on the z-axis. Visualizing *embeddings* allows us to see how close, or far in this case, misconceptions are from each other.

Teacher Education and Development ♦ 169

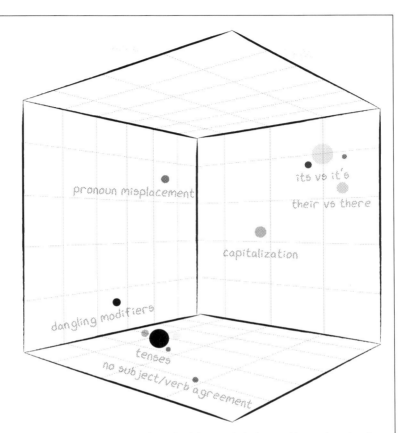

FIGURE 8.1 Example of embeddings (of three dimensions) of a few common misconceptions by English language learners in sentence construction. The larger the dot, the closer it is to the corner facing you. The less opaque the dot, the deeper it is on one of the dimensions. Each embedding could have many more dimensions, but it is impractical to visualize four dimensions or more on a flat piece of paper. Note how similar things, like "its vs it's" and "their vs they're" end up close to each other

Embeddings from misconceptions *cluster* similar misconceptions[8] and serve as a reliable way to organize a large gamut of misconceptions. Above, we can see a couple of *clusters* of misconceptions forming for "tenses" and "its vs it's."

> There are many techniques that help you make these *embeddings*, but a popular one used in the world of language is called **word2vec**.[9] This is a variation on *bag-of-words* and is made using a *neural network* (a detailed explanation is out of the scope of this section). *Embeddings* can be used as *inputs* to other *neural networks*.
>
> Regardless of the technique you use, having *embeddings* of misconceptions opens multiple possibilities for better preparing *models* that sequence learning experiences for students. For example, multiple pieces of knowledge whose misconceptions are *predicted* to be close to each other may be targeted by a single learning experience. This would translate to, for example, fewer activities in the classroom that yield the most enriching learning. Or even, simply, to allow a student to practice extensively on an identified misconception, a *model* could target similar misconceptions that form in the cluster around the one in focus.

If AI can *predict* misconceptions for a topic that a teacher is being trained to be proficient instructing in, it can be extremely useful to him/her in emulating and practicing planning. But, even more importantly, it can help create realistic in-classroom scenarios for specific content that teachers need to respond to in real-time. Such practice can emulate aspects of teacher residency programs, which are difficult to put together in the first place.

But I am sure you are also wondering how these authentic misconception scenarios are presented to teachers. Asking these *predictions* as questions on a written exam is useful, but they don't adequately prepare teachers to enhance their natural instructional response. So, while their curricular knowledge might improve, it wouldn't prepare them to respond in high-pressure classroom environments where teachers see very raw natural inputs of student faces, bodies, and sounds.

For example, if these same misconception scenarios are presented in an authentic way—say, having paid actors acting like how students would have responded to a lesson being taught by the teacher being trained—teachers can get a much richer practice opportunity in responding to real student struggles.

New vocabulary	Unfortunately, Hollywood aspirants aren't everywhere, so what is the very best we can do to give teachers the same surreal high-sensory experience? The most interesting development in building such experiences is **virtual reality** (VR). While not a branch of AI in its traditional focus, *virtual reality* creates real-ish simulated worlds and spaces—and in our case this could be classrooms—through headsets which trick the mind into believing the virtual to be real and elicit teachers' most natural human responses.
	Creating such virtual environments with virtual students acting out the *outputs* of misconception *models*—in response to a trainee teacher's speech and action, captured and recognized through headsets and sensors—can be endlessly improved, while being cost-effective. Alternatively, the trainee teacher can be an observer who can move freely, observing student work in a virtual space, watching a sample simulated teacher teach a lesson, and pausing to discuss these simulated teacher's challenges and options.
	All this can be done before teachers have to enter the high-stakes classroom environments, which aren't playgrounds anymore.

Tool to try	Mursion ($$$) is a *virtual reality* environment that trains teachers and other professionals in a simulated environment on critical skills needed to succeed before they enter the workplace. They see virtual students sitting in classrooms and get to encounter difficult classroom situations before they happen in real life.

Teacher education programs obviously teach so much more than trying to prepare you for student engagement time. This is merely one way AI can help in augmenting them.

"In-Service" Professional Development

"In-service" is the most common kind of professional development—the on-the-job kind. Here, we see slightly different challenges and opportunities since teachers have no dearth of in-person time with their students.

If we treat professional development as any other learning process, it offers us the same opportunities in engagement and relevance as any student-learning experience does with the advancements in *Intelligent Tutoring Systems*, except that it is the teachers who are the students here. *Intelligent Tutoring Systems*, combined with online mentorship and guidance from real advisers, can create very personalized human+AI experiences for learning. Professional development online courses are useful only if they target specific gaps in teacher knowledge, instead of being repetitively obvious.

New vocabulary	Professional development online courses may incorporate *collaborative filtering*, a technique we discussed before when talking about *recommendation systems*, to suggest content to teachers that their colleagues find most useful.

Tool to try	*Collaborative filtering* is popular in consumer culture on platforms like Netflix ($$$) for watching movies or TV and on Amazon.com ($$$) for products you may want to buy that are related to what you bought, because of what other people in your situation did.

But what evidence can such AI-powered professional development systems use to ascertain that teachers are putting their learning into practice in their classrooms? One of the age-old techniques to measure effectiveness of teaching is **classroom observations**. Where expert evaluators—usually subject heads or vice-principals, and sometimes external evaluators—spend time in every class and try to provide a subjective evaluation of the teacher's performance.

But human observation is not only exorbitantly expensive at scale,[10] it is also very error-prone and bias-prone. AI presents us with a few tools which, when combined, can allow us to observe the quality of teaching, analyze it in comparison to what great teaching looks like, and provide teachers with corrective steps.

New vocabulary	*Automatic Speech Recognition* with *speaker diarization* allows us to capture teacher and student speech, while *video tracking* with *affect detection* allows us to better understand student engagement during this process. Additionally, teacher and student movement can be *predicted* and understood through *activity recognition*.
	The resulting data can allow us to build *models* that can *predict* engagement in the classroom, and tied with ability to analyze the transcript of what was spoken, we can profile the coverage of *competencies* and *predict* the choices of activities and strategies.

An AI that can observe and make *predictions* much more often than a human evaluator can provide extensive analysis of what happened during the lesson to the teacher, both during and after every lesson wraps up. This may be like the information provided on a driving dashboard in a car: multiple scores about current performance given as instantaneous feedback so that he/she can adjust the lesson to reach the learning destination in the best possible manner, and then be told how it went to boost confidence and provide momentum to do even better the next time.

But this doesn't necessarily give a teacher clear remedies on how to change their teaching for the next lesson. It merely gives them a diagnosis of what went wrong. A system that consequently offers feedback on how to improve and keep the class on track would be much more useful.

New vocabulary	We know that using *Reinforcement Learning* here could be one way of preparing feedback. That's because if we can see that we are not going to get the most *reward* in the long term, we can tell the teacher which set of *actions* might do that.

But again, this needs a *model trained* on lots of examples of positive and negative *actions*. This is surely possible with student responses, but not easily with teaching *actions* because it is hard to come up with so much accurate data.

We may use a newer spin on *Reinforcement Learning* that is more appropriate to our needs, called **Imitation Learning**.[11] *Imitation learning* is exactly what it sounds like—AI that tries to imitate a sequence of actions performed by a human. So, imagine a computer being able to watch a few master teacher lessons, and *predict* the series of *states* in them. *Imitation Learning* is still in its early stages today but has a lot of promise for the future. |

Tool to try	FortressIQ ($$$) is a set of tools for organizations that help them automate repetitive tasks by imitating complex actions by employees and learning the behavior. Such actions are often hard to "codify" into rules in expert systems like business rules engines.

When a novice teacher teaches a lesson similar to what the AI has learned to be expert instruction, the AI can offer a suggestion on the next correct situation the teacher may wish to strive for and what choice of activity might lead there, to prevent the lesson from derailing.

On the other hand, there will likely be a sizable number of situations when experienced teachers will deliberately choose alternative pathways, and these will be the opportunities where the teacher can teach the AI to "imitate" less and learn from new perspectives.

Teacher Education and Development ◆ 175

> *New classrooms*
>
> Before teaching a unit or a textbook chapter, Ms. Wuku used to go through all the materials page-to-page and roughly figured out a pacing over a couple of weeks. Doing this a few times led her to realize that her ideal pacing often gets thrown off by students at different speeds, given their weaker prior knowledge on, and misconceptions from, past learning. She tried to fix this by trying to get a hold of prior year teachers and combing through prior student data that these teachers could share, but it was still hard to tell which content students would struggle with.
>
> Now, this problem has gone away. Ms. Wuku opens the misconceptions website on her laptop computer. When she enters some information on the skill or content she is teaching, the site lists all the possible misconceptions students might have from the past that makes it difficult for her to teach the new material. She then uses this knowledge by explicitly building up that prior knowledge before she introduces new content and skills.

Notes

1. Although I still find it very strange considering organizational mandate changes in other disciplines are not associated with so many overheads in new learning.
2. Darling-Hammond, L. (1985). Valuing teachers: The making of a profession. *Teachers College Record*, 87(2), 205–218.
3. Brown, J. S., & Burton, R. R. (1978). Diagnostic models for procedural bugs in basic mathematical skills. *Cognitive Science*, 2(2), 155–192.
4. Brown & Burton (1978).
5. Smith III, J. P., diSessa, A. A., & Roschelle, J. (1994). Misconceptions reconceived: A constructivist analysis of knowledge in transition. *Journal of the Learning Sciences*, 3(2), 115–163.
6. Mikolov, T., Sutskever, I., Chen, K., Corrado, G., & Dean, J. (2013). Distributed representations of words and phrases and their

compositionality. *Proceedings of the 26th International Conference on Neural Information Processing Systems—Volume 2* (pp. 3111–3119).
 7 Bordes, A., Weston, J., Collobert, R., & Bengio, Y. (2011). Learning structured embeddings of knowledge bases. *Proceedings of the AAAI Conference on Artificial Intelligence*, 25(1). Retrieved from https://ojs.aaai.org/index.php/AAAI/article/view/7917.
 8 Pardos, Z., Farrar, S., Kolb, J., Peh, G. X., & Lee, J. H. (2018). Distributed representation of misconceptions. In J. Kay and R. Luckin (Eds.), *Rethinking learning in the digital age: Making the learning sciences count, 13th International Conference of the Learning Sciences (ICLS) 2018, Volume 3*. London, UK: International Society of the Learning Sciences.
 9 Mikolov, T., Chen, K., Corrado, G., & Dean, J. (2013). Efficient estimation of word representations in vector space. In *1st International Conference on Learning Representations, ICLR 2013*, Scottsdale, Arizona, USA, May 2–4, 2013, Workshop Track Proceedings.
10 Kane, T. (2012). Capturing the dimensions of effective teaching: Student achievement gains, student surveys, and classroom observations. *Education Next*, 12(4), 34+.
11 Hussein, A., Gaber, M. M., Elyan, E., & Jayne, C. (2017). Imitation learning: A survey of learning methods. *ACM Computing Surveys (CSUR)*, 50(2), 1–35.

9
Challenges

There are a large number of talent, capital, and market challenges involved in bringing the kind of AI discussed so far to classrooms. But I don't want to focus on those. There is also unjustified pessimism towards this field because you may know of a company or two in San Francisco that has already tried bringing one of these ideas to fruition, but they haven't worked out so far. I am not going to spend time discussing that either. Having said that, one thing I will share is that I am a believer in the power of competition driving more innovation but, unfortunately, there are just not enough high-efficacy technology makers in education today.

Instead, I want to discuss the hurdles in bringing these technologies to life. The AI-savvy reader could not have gotten to this section without constantly raising an eyebrow about one or more of these imminent elephants in the room:

- Lack of enough data
- Accuracy
- Domain-specific research

Let's discuss them one at a time.

Lack of Enough Data

Intuitively, this seems strange: there is data everywhere—millions of kids around the world trying to solve tens of millions of exercises every day and millions of hours of lesson time—yet there is not enough data for us to *train models* with. Such large numbers of students exhibit similar learning traits, using the exact same national or state mandated curriculum—yet, securing a significant number of students' longitudinal response and performance data anonymously? Not happening![1]

For context on how things could be, it's important to know that many of the publicly reproducible data-hungry advancements in AI have come from work on openly available *datasets* sponsored by "noble" technology leaders. Industry and academia peers benchmark algorithmic progress using these *datasets*, for consistency. Companies and research labs understand that if everyone is better off, then *they* are surely going to be better off. That said, there are enough examples of large tech companies building superior AI because of the "proprietary" user data they have access to. Which, apart from delayed publishing of most important internal research, gives their products an edge over their competitors' products.

In yet another practice of securing high-quality data, products whose core value proposition revolves around their AI capabilities, end up appearing in the market simpler and cheaper than what they can be. They do this for "strategic data acquisition," which Andrew Ng[2] describes as a recurring 3-step loop: build a simpler product, acquire some data, and then refine the product using the data. And then continue with building more of the product.

| *Tool to try* | Common Voice ($$$) is an initiative by Mozilla, the nonprofit that builds the web-browser Firefox. Its objective is to build the largest *dataset* of *labeled* voice samples of humans reading statements of text, to empower *Automatic Speech Recognition* systems. It is a new community-first paradigm in how data can be collected and shared; rather than independently paying people to record readings of pieces of text and use the data only on their systems, the initiative allows anyone with a browser to record, label, and review voice samples. All the recorded sounds and their matching labels are published openly for anyone to use for free. |

So where has data come from in the advancements we have made so far in the classroom in *modeling* students? You guessed it right—companies, academic researchers, and product makers have had to rely on the limited data from within their own products and research experiments. But what if you just do research and don't make products? Tough luck for you. What if you can form a partnership with multiple schools and get their parents on board? This is much more difficult in practice than it sounds, but considering you manage to do this, that still might be too little data because of how data-hungry many of the techniques we discussed earlier are.

| *Tool to try* | Carnegie Mellon University's LearnLab, an institute focused on the science around learning, runs the largest online data repository of learning interaction data called DataShop ($$$). Anonymized data from many prior learning experiments with students, primarily through digital interaction systems, is available for further research and experimentation. |

The Problem With Too Little Data

But "what's the problem with too little data?" you ask. There are a lot of problems with too little data. *Training models* with little data lead to a problem a statistician may refer to as **overfitting**. *Overfitting* means that the *model* or *function* that has been optimized best responds to *inputs* similar to what it was *trained* on, and not *inputs* that look different and also occur naturally.

Here's a substandard analogy: say you open a new clothing brand. You live in a fictitious country called Vyatland where the median height is fairly short, say 5'2," because of the diets of your ancestors. You want to make clothes for everyone in the world, but all the data points that you have around you tell you that people are generally short. You make some t-shirts. These fit the locals perfectly. But your audience is international, and the moment you ship t-shirts to Nordic countries, nobody can wear them because they are too small. You just *overfit* your production lines to the people of Vyatland, and that stops you from becoming a brand for everyone around the world. *Overfitting* gives you, what a statistics student would call, "high variance and low bias."[3]

Alternative Approaches

But too little data might not turn out to be the end of the road. It turns out that teaching and learning is not the only area in which data is "sparse"—the commonly used adjective to describe small and shoddy *datasets*. This concern across multiple fields has led researchers in *machine learning* to begin to put in energy to come up with techniques that are more "sample efficient," that is, that can create a similar fidelity of *models* with a small amount of *training* data, or learn things in, for example, a "single shot," that is, without multiple examples of the same thing.[4] But this remains an open problem.

It is vital that when we think about gathering data, we think carefully about which range of subjects and grades we intend to build AI around, and if the data other people have collected can work for our needs. Today, existing datasets come from very specialized AI-based teaching and learning *tutoring systems* for a subset of topics in a subject, for example, learning algebra or trigonometry.

New vocabulary	From historical experience, we know that acquiring significant amounts of data to build *models* of a student's knowledge construction across the wide world of ever-expanding content of different subjects is somewhat unrealistic because of expense, privacy, and logistics.
	Other problems in *machine learning* have found themselves at a similar place. Think about the self-driving car problem. All around the world, even though cars look more or less the same, the road rules and conditions they are driven in are not the same. A one-size-fits-all *model* for determining how to steer the wheel does not work. Each unique combination of road rules and conditions needs a little fine-tuning over a largely common general *prediction*-making system. But it seems unrealistic to collect large amounts of such driving data in every small town around the world.
	This has given rise to a set of techniques known as **transfer learning**, where existing *models*, or parts of them, prepared with ample data in one domain, can be reused on newer problems that exhibit similar properties.[5] This is done by determining which parts of the *neural network* are common between the two problems, preserving them, and then *training* and refining only the parts that are unique to the new problem. This depends on much less data. But this is not very easy to do.
	Transfer learning lends itself well to *modeling* teaching and learning of content across different sub-domains and depths of a single subject, or in subjects whose underlying learning and pedagogical principles are similar, for example, in language learning.

Lastly, there is also a whole slew of creative solutions[6] being worked on to keep the privacy of such data intact so it cannot be abused by a technology powerhouse, while at the same time allowing AI to be built for a better future.

Accuracy

Mis-tagging a face in a Facebook photo has relatively negligible consequences. Alexa not understanding you the first couple of times: no problemo! But misunderstanding even a single student's needs at a critical learning juncture can push you into shaping instruction that forever turns off his/her interest in that topic. Needless to say, the stakes are much higher in teaching and learning, and the levels of accuracy (the way quality is measured and evaluated) that modern AI-based consumer products are built with don't cut it in "mission-critical" settings like classrooms. Working eight out of ten times is often just not enough. And that success rate—80 percent—is already considered rather high on many of the problems with breakthrough AI solutions in the past few years. And that's not even considering that not working has worse than neutral consequences; every intervention and experiment directly affects the memory of real humans in already scarce classroom instruction time.

And then we have the issue of not having a great plan to understand the truest needs of the students. This is a consequence of the fact that most AI research focuses on making computers learn to do what humans do well and getting humans out of the way. But AI for teaching and learning should emphasize the opposite: **making human learning optimal**. Something that we struggle to measure in any reasonable depth. Our best shot at this, as discussed above, has been *student/learner modeling*. Our ways to *model* students so far have been fairly shallow and incomplete *representations* of what is likely a much more complex process.[7] Simple diagnostic assessments that we use in initializing these *models* often don't capture aspects like prior knowledge, readiness, latent misconceptions, metacognitive skills, and other cues in interpersonal and social skills.

Apart from being shallow and incomplete, our ways to *model* students using AI can sometimes be "unfair" if we are not careful about the implications of the assumptions in the algorithms and data that make up the techniques. "Unfair" here, and in the context of *machine learning* which makes *predictions* on human behavior, knowledge, or activity in general, means being inequitable in a way that eventually leads to a disadvantage for a person or a group of people as a result of decisions made based on *predictions*. This isn't just hypothetical; in research experiments, researchers of *student modeling* found that *knowledge tracing models* wrongly *predicted* that lower-performing students were on par with other students in terms of mastery of the material.[8]

Bridging the "Inaccuracy Gap"

Until we achieve a higher-level of accuracy and better *student modeling*, we will need to design solutions where humans bridge the "inaccuracy gap" while allowing AI to do a large amount of heavy lifting. By bridging the "inaccuracy gap," I mean doing the work that the AI would have done had it been highly accurate, while still allowing it to do the pattern recognition it is very good at that doesn't involve deeply understanding teaching and learning.

For example, the AI might *predict* that a student is going to be able to ace a reading comprehension of new piece of informational text because he/she has done rather well on reading assignments of this level of text complexity so far. But it might not consider that most practice reading comprehensions done by the student so far required readings around content that the student was loosely familiar with, and that the new reading might be from a complex technical domain which will throw the student off. To prevent this, the designers of this AI may have to work with reading coaches to mitigate such speed bumps, before offering the solution to schools.

Perhaps the AI research community, guided by educators, might realize at some point that *neural networks* may not be the best toolkit for so many of our problems after all, and that's completely okay. The techniques we use are bound to change, as long as we are sincere about the quality of learning we wish to enable, with AI by our side.

Domain-specific Research

Closely related to accuracy is the notion of **generalizability**. *Generalizability* means the ability to work in more general, non-specific scenarios.

In the descriptions of many things in AI discussed in earlier chapters, you may have observed the use of words like "technique," "problem area," and "sub-field," instead of "solution" or "tool." That's because a lot of the technological research and progress on AI has happened in contexts different from the physical *screen-less* K–12 classroom environment we have been focusing on throughout the book. So, a lot of these are still just big ideas in teaching and learning today.

A lot of this success has come from non-classroom environments in domains with different characteristics and needs. Speech research may be driven by home assistant device makers, voice research by phone assistants, and vision research by social media companies tagging pictures. Long-term rewards research has been designed in emulated worlds with physics engines for making robots great. *NLP* direction is set forward by search engines. None of these are going to magically work great for teaching and learning on Day 1 of implementation.

Even a lot of success in the *knowledge tracing* world has come from data being captured in interactive student response systems on screens for extended digital learning sessions, and not in click-less teacher interactions with an informed human in control of workflow.

Succeeding in Screen-less Environments

To truly succeed in the *screen-less* classroom learning environments, this very research would need to, at least partially, be driven within the constraints and affordances of students, teachers, classrooms, and brick-and-mortar schools. This is going to be the source of new discoveries, practices, and perspectives.

As I mentioned before, what makes AI research for teaching and learning fundamentally distinct is our goal of uncovering and making human learning optimal. And this means that the teacher using the technology—and not a researcher sitting in a Silicon Valley theme park—will need to constantly interpret numbers generated during the process of the machine's understanding of what's going on in a student's mind and why it recommends one teacher action over another (through what may sometimes be called a **pedagogy model**[9]).

Despite having recommendations from the AI, concerned teachers will naturally worry about the integrity of the insides of these mathematical *models*. They may ask: "is the reasoning used by these formulae or algorithms something I agree with?" And it doesn't stop at teachers. In recent times, there has been an increasing focus on student awareness and control in their learning journey.[10] So, students would and should be highly interested in this understanding for their own growth.

Today, the number-crunching going on in mathematically dense techniques like *deep learning* wouldn't make much sense to most researchers easily, leave alone teachers. Unfortunately, due to the nature of *deep learning*, the *representations* that make up the *models* have very **low interpretability**. This simply means that it is very hard, even for the people building these AI systems, to understand the hidden *functions* and *layers* that represent this information. Solving this type of problem is the focus of an area called **explainable AI**.[11]

This idea of *explainable AI*, along with the issues of fairness and transparency, fall under the general umbrella of "Fairness, Accountability, and Transparency" in *machine learning*.[12] For the day to come when teachers can understand the "reasoning" of algorithms in AI's techniques, a lot of these numbers would need to be communicated in a language they would understand. This would require several educators to be embedded into a complex loop of *human–computer interaction* AFTER the scientists figure out how to extract and summarize the reasons that pushed the machines to make a specific *prediction*, among many options. This is not possible without an explicit focus on such domain-specific research, the domain being teaching and learning in *screen-less* environments. Fortunately for us, some of these environments are the contexts of research and progress in the young field of *multimodal learning analytics* that we touched upon earlier.

Putting Educators-in-the-Loop
Teachers may have a little more work cut out for them, apart from just trying to understand the "reasoning" inside computer's minds. Teachers might be needed to help computers understand what just happened with the data the computers just acquired in the middle of *training* processes. This is when researchers building these systems will involve *experts* or *humans-in-the-loop*, ideas we touched on before. With enough expert understanding built on these complete tasks, the need for humans to hand-hold the system will slowly become less and less.

Here's a couple of futuristic examples of what this might end up looking like in practice:

1. A civics teacher asks her students to write an argumentative piece on the rights of refugees in a country. After grading writing style, structure, and cohesiveness of the argument, the AI is "confused" on how to comprehend the effectiveness of a student's claim about the prospective value of giving large labor rights to refugees, because it has never seen cases of such a dynamic played out. Nor has the teacher seen anything like this. But the teacher has amassed a complex multi-dimensional dynamic understanding of the world and a very human instinct of evaluating humankind, and so, he/she could nudge the AI into his/her train of thought.
2. A theater teacher needs to go through a large number of auditions of students to determine which students will play what parts. To avoid taking days to do this, she

finds an AI that *predicts* the quality of a theatrical performance from video and sound *input*. She asks hundreds of students across grades to take this audition on their phones or in an audio/visual lab at school. When the AI comes across a certain facial twitch and doesn't know how to *classify* it, it may ask the teacher for her opinion based on his/her experiences of spending a long career in the theater industry seeing innovative new expressions.

3. In listening to student speech in the classroom, an AI identifies the distinct sound of a student who recently joined from a minority community. Since the AI might have never come across those speech characteristics in the data it is *trained* on, it might be "tempted" to *classify* that speech as a distraction to classmates, and consequently alert the teacher. Before doing so, it may confer with the teacher on whether this sound is intentionally ill-mannered, or completely natural.

These very situations may arise well before it even goes into practice, when a teacher is *training* a system using prior data to be ready for a large number of scenarios.

| Tool to try | Teachers guiding an AI system to be better at understanding student work isn't all futuristic. We discussed earlier how successes in *Intelligent Tutoring Systems* have helped us *model* student learning. One of the key components needed to make a non-topic specific *Intelligent Tutoring System* is an ***expert* model**.[13] This, as you may guess, is knowledge in the system of how the various pieces of learning in the topic are structured. This is a knowledge-based AI kind of *model*. A teacher would need to know how to program in an AI programming language to create this model before the system can build a *model* of a student's learning. But let's be real: it's unrealistic to expect many teachers who learn AI programming to be able to take advantage of such a system. |

> It would be amazing if AI could be used to make an *expert model* out of the structure of various pieces of learning in the topic from the expert teacher's guidance, before turning it into an *Intelligent Tutoring System* for students. SimStudent ($$$) is a machine learning agent that does exactly that. By posing problems and providing feedback on the steps taken by the agent OR by demonstrating the right steps in performing a learning task, a teacher can build an *expert model* using SimStudent, taking him/her one step closer to having an *Intelligent Tutoring System* for the topic.

But solving these tasks, which I can imagine will involve skills of empathy, argumentation, wisdom, and extensive practice, and more of what we attribute as enablers to very higher-order thinking and reasoning skills, likely won't be the priority of many other groups than the education community. And when I say education community, I mean people who teach and learn actively day-in and day-out, and not in the general "we are all learners" sense. So actively making such research a priority is critical.

Conclusion: Building a Case for AI

These challenges will take many, many years, possibly decades, to solve. We cannot be too sure of how much computing technology would have entered classrooms, to be able to harness AI's capabilities, by the day when we have the best solutions that understand every student's learning and emotional needs. Especially given how low the technology penetration in classrooms across the world is today, we will have to make a strong case for it.

I believe that the most obvious reason why most schools don't utilize more computing, in the form of laptops, video conference cameras, smartboards/screens, tablets, etc., in the classroom is because these devices don't solve many problems for teaching and learning today, in comparison to the cost and effort people have to take to install them and keep them working. Small governments across the world avoid placing computers in every public-school classroom, not because they don't have the money, but because there isn't a strong enough case for these devices to budget for them. Every decision for budget planners and financiers of the world revolves around cost and benefit, and if the cost is much greater than the benefit, it's a no-go.

I believe technologies that will overcome some of these AI-for-teaching-learning-improvement challenges, and create products that reliably improve learning outcomes, will make decisions around buying hardware, software, cellular data connections, etc. a no-brainer. I hope that when such a time arrives, student success is celebrated far more than technology purchases.

Notes

1 Read this story for one perspective: Horn, M. (2014). "InBloom's collapse offers lessons for innovation in education." *Forbes Magazine*, December 4. Retrieved from www.forbes.com/sites/michaelhorn/2014/12/04/inblooms-collapse-offers-lessons-for-innovation-in-education/#1a1d8217525f.
2 Ng. A. (n.d.). *The state of artificial intelligence*. Retrieved May 18, 2021 from www.youtube.com/watch?v=NKpuX_yzdYs.
3 Ramzai, J. (2019, February 21). Holy grail for bias-variance tradeoff, overfitting & underfitting. *Medium*. Retrieved from https://juhiramzai.medium.com/holy-grail-for-bias-variance-tradeoff-overfitting-underfitting-7fad64ab5d76.
4 Vinyals, O., Blundell, C., Lillicrap, T., Kavukcuoglu, K., & Wierstra, D. (2016). Matching networks for one shot learning. *Proceedings of the 30th International Conference on Neural Information Processing Systems*, 3637–3645.
5 Pan, S. J., & Yang, Q. (2009). A survey on transfer learning. *IEEE Transactions on Knowledge and Data Engineering*, 22(10), 1345–1359.
6 For example, Differential Privacy, which, according to Harvard University Privacy Tools Project, states that "an algorithm is said to

be differentially private if by looking at the output, one cannot tell whether any individual's data was included in the original dataset or not. In other words, the guarantee of a differentially private algorithm is that its behavior hardly changes when a single individual joins or leaves the dataset—anything the algorithm might output on a database containing some individual's information is almost as likely to have come from a database without that individual's information."

7 Tuomi, I., Cabrera, M., Vuorikari, R., Punie, Y., Europäische Kommission, & Gemeinsame Forschungsstelle (2018). *The impact of artificial intelligence on learning, teaching, and education policies for the future.* Retrieved from https://doi.org/10.2760/12297.

8 Doroudi, S., & Brunskill, E. (2019). Fairer but not fair enough on the equitability of knowledge tracing. *Proceedings of the 9th International Conference on Learning Analytics & Knowledge*, 335–339. Retrieved from https://doi.org/10.1145/3303772.3303838.

9 Graesser, A., Brawner, K., Sottilare, R., & Hu, X. (2015). *Design recommendations for intelligent tutoring systems: Authoring tools and expert modeling techniques.* Adelphi, MD: Army Research Laboratory.

10 Russ, R. S., Sherin, B. L., & Sherin, M. G. (2016). What constitutes teacher learning. *Handbook of Research on Teaching*, 391–438.

11 Samek, W., Montavon, G., Vedaldi, A., Hansen, L. K., & Müller, K.-R. (Eds.) (2019). *Explainable AI: Interpreting, explaining and visualizing deep learning.* New York: Springer International Publishing. Retrieved from https://doi.org/10.1007/978-3-030-28954-6.

12 *FAT ML* (n.d.). Retrieved May 24, 2021 from www.fatml.org/.

13 Matsuda, N., Cohen, W. W., & Koedinger, K. R. (2015). Teaching the teacher: Tutoring Simstudent leads to more effective cognitive tutor authoring. *International Journal of Artificial Intelligence in Education*, 25(1), 1–34.

10
Getting Started With Making New AI Innovations

In the likelihood that you haven't been dissuaded by the challenges, and are brave and brimming with an idea or two that involves AI to improve teaching and learning in your school or education system at large, this chapter is for you. If you don't have any such ideas, that is completely okay. Understanding developments in AI should ideally only magnify a burning desire for an innovative idea you have had for a long time, but didn't think the technology was there for it yet. Try not to solve a non-existent problem for AI's sake.

Your idea could be a new initiative, an audit, a market survey, an app idea, a larger software or hardware system, or an area of scientific exploration. It doesn't have to involve anyone building new technology. But if it does, it could be as basic as putting together existing AI-based tools using a few hours of technology development, or as complicated as a brand-new research problem that will take a long time to solve. And you don't have to be alone in solving it; the best kinds of AI projects bring together collaborators from multiple disciplines.

Since you may not have done something like this before, the upcoming sections highlight some of the essential steps you may take to help you get started on this journey and avoid making common pitfalls. There is no perfect formula, nor are these directions from start to finish; every project is going to apply them in a unique way. Also, I am not assuming that you know how to build a technology tool. Regardless, the upcoming sections serve as important considerations for people you end up working with.

Start With an Authentic Problem

In a fear of stating the obvious and patronizing, neither being my intention, I'll keep this short. Your deep dive into creating something using AI should be driven by a very real problem that could alleviate a huge amount of pain or dramatically change the learning experience in your classroom. Taking this deep dive into creating something using AI shouldn't happen just because you are interested in a cool AI capability that is in search of a problem.

Why? Because it will eat up time that you could allocate to other worthy endeavors. And it's a whole lot more work than you think. That's because putting together a novel AI innovation is very much unlike putting together a simple mobile or desktop application or creating a website, which your software developer friend said would take only a handful of days to make. Making a novel AI innovation takes a lot of trial and experimentation, depending on what you are going for. And for reasons we will soon discuss, this trial and experimentation process is extremely expensive.

But this is less of a problem if your idea is going to create immense value.

So, how do you tell if your idea is going to create immense value? You work in a uniquely interesting profession where you are surrounded by the beneficiaries of the value you create. These beneficiaries are your students. You also spend a lot of time with your peers discussing difficulties you face. So just get feedback from students **or** run little safe and creative experiments to figure this one out.

For example, say you are excited about the potential of putting together AI technology that will *predict* how tired your students are during any class period. To determine the value of how this will change your colleagues' approach to instruction or class scheduling, you put together a little experiment. You ask students to answer a question about their energy levels in their paper exit ticket at the end of each period on a class day. Share this information with all the staff at a meeting and try to recognize patterns on what might be going on, using the records on instructional activities from lesson plans, student performance, and their tiredness levels. Then act on these patterns, with an intervention in the lesson or duration of class periods and measure the impact they have in higher student engagement and outcomes.

New vocabulary	Alternatively, for testing the prospects of a system where users interact with a system, you may use a specific technique. This technique is used by designers of intelligent systems and *human–computer interactions* to quickly get feedback and gauge potential value of a system that acts and behaves like the real thing. It is called the **Wizard of Oz** technique,[1] and you may try using this with your idea.
	It works this way: say you wish to make a system that depends on a specific AI capability existing. You invite a potential user of the technology to interact with a paper or less-sophisticated technology version (think drawings on PowerPoint slides), and he/she begins engaging with your system. The text, words, actions, or visuals of the person engaging with the system are somehow sent over to another person (our "wizard") sitting in another room, through your choice of camera and microphone technologies. This wizard presumably has at least the level of intelligence of the AI you wish to create. The wizard does the expected task for the user, and the user's desires are ideally met without realizing that a human performed these tasks. You can, at this stage, ask questions about how much the user valued the AI capability to gauge if this is going to be highly valuable.

Simplify Your Innovation to the "Minimum Viable AI"

In case you are not writing an AI ethics policy proposal for your school, your idea at this point probably looks a lot like an app or website which does something with student data and then gives you and other teachers some *predictions* in a user interface, which makes it easy for them to understand these results.

Unfortunately, trying to bring such innovations to life, often with the assistance of more programming-savvy people, is going to take an enormous amount of time and money. To the point that, if it doesn't go exactly according to plan, it may discourage you from wanting to try innovative things in the future. We don't want that. This is so common in the world of building innovative technologies, that there is a best practice of first coming up with a significantly simplified bare-bones version called the *Minimum Viable Product*, which is cheap and does not destroy a maker's emotions and bank accounts.[2]

Adding AI to the mix makes things a little more complicated. The stakes are even higher for the following three reasons:

- **Human capital**: The number of people in this world today who are capable of building truly innovative AI technology is very small, and therefore, they are much more sought after. They also need a lot of time in the trial and experimentation process. This makes the process very exorbitantly expensive. Unless you spend a few years immersed in learning how to do this scientific research yourself, you will need to depend on such people, who often charge top dollar.
- **Computation cost**: The cost of running an innovative technology is dependent on the amount of mathematical calculations a computer needs to do, apart from other factors. Unlike most technology applications that use computers with Central Processing Units (CPUs—the

primary chips that are the basis of most computing and which are relatively affordable), AI-based applications often depend on computers with more expensive Graphics Processing Units (GPUs) for *training* models and eventually making *predictions*. These devices use enormous amounts of energy, translating to high cost of electricity.

- **Data acquisition, preparation, and storage**: We've already discussed how hard it is to acquire data. When organizations, both large and small, need data, but don't have the means to acquire it themselves, they spend a lot of money to acquire it from companies who sell it in bulk. The harder the data is to acquire, the more expensive it is. It then often needs to be cleaned up using data engineering steps and stored on large hard disks. A very small percentage of lucky schools with data analysts/scientists on staff may make some of these steps easier.

So, you must try to start with simplifying the first version of your innovative ideas down to, what I call, a **Minimum Viable AI**; just the bare-bones of what will prove to the larger community that if your idea is given more support, it can really impact learning outcomes or student wellness to a large extent.

How might you do that? Here are a couple of things you may consider doing to arrive at your *Minimum Viable AI* idea:

1. **Break down constituent pieces**: Break down your larger idea into the small pieces it is made up of. Remove anything that does not seem as important. In this process, you should consider eliminating the common functionalities that are found in apps or tools popularly available that don't directly improve teaching and learning. Get rid of login screens, dashboards, nice user interfaces, and other customizations that allow for many kinds of *predictions*.

You will be left with the bare-bones. This will require some manual data entry or painful *labeling* and no user interface. But what will remain is where your magic will lie.

2. **Think about whether or not teacher time is the bottleneck**: Ask yourself: "is lack of limitless time that teachers can allocate the reason this learning problem is not solved?" If the answer is yes, and your idea can essentially allow for AI to be a substitute for that hard-to-acquire teacher time, you are on the right track. If not, AI might not be the solution to the problem you are looking at.

Determine the Data or Knowledge Needs

What you can't capture in the form of data, you can't make *predictions* or individualized suggestions on. And sometimes, capturing the data or knowledge needed is simply not possible in the logistical and regulatory environments we teach our students in. So, it is vitally important to figure out how you will either capture the data to build a *model*, or how you might eventually feed it with *inputs* to make *predictions* in the moment. If you can manage to capture data for *training*, and eventually make *predictions* on unseen data, it is also extremely crucial that you **pay close attention to making sure that the privacy of the data you collect cannot be compromised by a bad actor**. Depending on where you live, there may be different legal requirements that you have to keep in mind and plan for. Regardless, as a bare minimum, you must remove any "personally identifiable information" associated with any data you collect, to anonymize it. Anonymizing it means that a person or computerized system which gets access to your system, with or without permission, cannot trace any single piece of data back to the individual whose data it is. You may do this by ensuring that any piece of data linked to a student is linked to a unique identifier, which possibly comes from another secure system where student information is managed, and not a student's name, location/address, email address, state/national ID number, etc. Nothing should be used that can be used to track down the person.

Of course, it would be wonderful to be able to capture or acquire all the right data to create a mathematical kind of AI, the one we have mostly talked about in most parts of the book that involve statistical approaches. But if you cannot capture a substantial amount of data to build *models* with, you can try to get creative with data acquisition over a longer period of time, as we discussed earlier in Chapter 9, our *Challenges* chapter. In a complete inability to capture data, you may consider putting together a non-mathematical kind where you tap into teachers as *humans-in-the-loop* or build an *expert system* with the knowledge of the specific domain. For example, if your AI revolves around literacy instruction, this knowledge could be based on the past two decades of literacy research documents. If it is based on helping students revise for history examinations, the knowledge could be captured from encyclopedias or primary sources. As it turns out often in teaching and learning, the mathematical kind and the non-mathematical kind complement and don't compete with one another. That said, it isn't trivial to design systems that harmoniously and seamlessly transition between the mathematical kind and the non-mathematical kind.

Consider the possibility of involving other people, at your school or in your community, in discussions around getting this data and doing good things with it. Spending time to think deeply about these matters builds a shared appreciation for the complexity of data policies and AI ethics in general.

Find Existing AI Offerings That You Can Use

The place where I recommend you spend most of your energy and time is in finding existing AI offerings that have already done the difficult work for you. By "difficult work," I mean work done by people to get access to a significant amount of data, experiment to find the right *machine learning* techniques and architectures, and consequently *train models* that are ready to make *predictions*.

If the AI element of your idea is closely related, or incrementally builds on the techniques we have discussed in this book that aren't necessarily tied to teaching and learning problems, you are more likely to find ready-made offerings. To find such offerings, you may begin with the key terms and phrases of techniques and capabilities that have been discussed all throughout this book. For example, if your idea for an AI innovation is a system that analyzes small-group discussions and tries to *predict* how much each student contributed verbally, you may begin your online search with: "automatic speech recognition," "deep learning," "speaker diarization," and "speaker separation."

This search will most often give you research articles and/or datasets. Such datasets may also be easily found by using Google's unique dataset search engine. You may or may not want that. What you want in the form of an existing offering, depending on how unique the problem you are trying to solve is, may be one of the following:

- **A tool with a user interface**: These are full ready-made apps and websites that give you an easy way to upload data from spreadsheets, images, audio files, or video files, and make the right *prediction* for you. Some examples have been shared in this book, like Dropbox, TurnItIn, TeachFX, Descript, Quill, and more.
- **A service with an "API"**: Other times, you may want these AI capabilities in YOUR app or website. Or maybe it's just that the user interfaces available do not work with your workflow and make life too cumbersome. In such cases, you are looking for an "Application Programming Interface" (API) to an AI service. This allows any software developer with no knowledge of AI to bring that capability into their innovative app or website. Many services provide such

APIs, including, but not limited to, Amazon Web Services, Google Cloud, IBM Watson, and Microsoft Azure.

- A *pre-trained model*: Often, on more niche problems with specific needs, scientists make the *trained models* available on the Internet. However, unlike with both previous kinds of offerings, it isn't entirely trivial to make *predictions* using these downloadable *model* files. Nonetheless, a "machine learning engineer," a special kind of software developer, can take a *model* and help you make an app or website that uses it to make *predictions*. An example of such a *pre-trained model* is a *language model*, the thing that *predicts* word(s) after a given word, and can be found on the Internet.
- A **software program**: More commonly available on the Internet, than *pre-trained models*, are new architectures in the form of bundles of code of the software program that build the *models*, put up by scientists and enthusiasts working on the code for novel *machine learning* problems. You are extremely likely to see these programs with some installation instructions on an online repository website called "GitHub," when searching online. These either come with some sample data to *train* with, or require you to bring your own data, depending on how unique or how *generalizable* the *model* needs to be.

Piggybacking on the discussion in the *Challenges* section, it's important to note that, just because someone offers the technology, that doesn't mean that it works well for your needs. So, it is imperative that you try and test it with the help of a "software developer" or "machine learning engineer," with what you plan to provide as *input data*.

Also, remember that if you are unable to find a *model* for your specific *data-based AI* problem, you may always explore the use of *transfer learning*, a topic we discussed earlier that allows you to adapt *models* from similar problems, to update an existing *model* to your needs.

There is a decent chance you have a novel or niche idea that no one has done research on and you are unsuccessful in finding ready-made offerings. In that case, you resort to the last step.

Invite Scientists to Your Challenges

If you have gone through vetting your idea with colleagues and friends, determined it to be of high importance, phrased it clearly in the language of AI, and are still unable to find existing offerings on it, it is a good time to ask:

> Does my idea feel feasible given the limited cognitive abilities of AI today? Or does my idea depend on a *general* AI?

If you come out of that believing it is practical and possible in the parameters of current advancements in AI, this might be a good time to share your idea with the world and welcome a community of scientists to consider spending some energy to think about it. Unlike traditional software development processes like apps, websites, and platforms, advancements and discoveries in *machine learning* are not always easy to figure out by one person or a small team in isolation.

There is no guarantee of success on whether your problem will be exciting to the scientific community at large. However, if you articulate the problem and it's expected impact well and using the right AI terminology, explaining the shortcomings of existing approaches, and present the problem at the right avenues like appropriate conferences, blogs, Kaggle.com, etc., you can significantly increase the likelihood of getting people excited about the problem. Here is a list of a few potential annual conference avenues for such a proposal:

- ◆ International Conference on Artificial Intelligence in Education

- International Conference on Learning Analytics & Knowledge
- Learning @ Scale Conference
- International Conference of the Learning Sciences
- International Conference on Education Data Mining
- Conference of Educational Data Mining
- Knowledge Discovery and Data Mining

One way to get the community involved in building AI solutions to unsolved problems has been to offer open competitions. In the past, competitions like the following have brought in stakeholders from across the community to solve specific challenging problems:

- In 2010, a competition at the Knowledge Discovery and Data Mining conference called the KDD Cup, was aimed at *predicting* student performance on mathematics problems based on historical student interaction data.[3]
- In 2017, a competition called the ASSISTments Longitudinal Data Competition at the Conference of Educational Data Mining, was aimed at *predicting* longitudinal (statistics-speak for long-term) outcomes, for example college and early career success, based on student performance data in middle school.[4]
- In 2018, the second-language acquisition mobile app Duolingo hosted a competition at the North American Chapter of the Association for Computational Linguistics conference to *predict* what mistakes a student will make in the future during the process of language learning, based on data of historical mistakes by them and others.[5]

More such collaborations between educators like yourself and AI research scientists will be extremely exciting, because of how much potential they have in improving teaching and learning.

Notes

1 Dahlbäck, N., Jönsson, A., & Ahrenberg, L. (1993). Wizard of Oz studies—why and how. *Knowledge-based Systems*, 6(4), 258–266.
2 Ries, E. (2011). *The lean startup: How today's entrepreneurs use continuous innovation to create radically successful businesses* (1st edn). New York: Crown Business.
3 See www.kdd.org/kdd-cup/view/kdd-cup-2010-student-performance-evaluation.
4 See https://sites.google.com/view/assistmentsdatamining.
5 See http://sharedtask.duolingo.com/.

11
Future

Perhaps even more influential than the vision for a field of human advancement is the **way the people working on it approach the vision**. AI was originally conceived as an interdisciplinary field based in psychology (which also happens to be where it was first published about[1]), philosophy, linguistics, applied mathematics (better known today as computer science), and more[2]—all working together to make machines think and act more like humans, often with a goal of alleviating repetitive human tasks. Understanding human learning was meant to be a precursor, and not an afterthought. And, coincidentally, some of these were the very same disciplines which formed some of our most foundational knowledge and perspective on teaching and learning.

But along the way, fearless statisticians and mathematicians steered towards the easily quantifiable, and consequently allowed a large amount of numerical data points be their guiding

DOI: 10.4324/9781003183235-11

light. Slowly, but unintentionally, as long as the algorithms did a decent job at solving sub-tasks, human intervention became a burden. What the *predictions* on data could tell us became more important than what and how the humans truly wanted to know. In the process, we have ended up with *machine learning*-powered AI that is only loosely related to what we know about how humans think.

The age-old dream of personalized learning paved the path for adaptive *Intelligent Tutoring Systems*, which sometimes distanced the teacher, at the expense of a vision for better learning. But after a series of humbling experiences, we may be arriving at the realization that a teacher, augmented with insights from AI—like a Teaching Assistant (TA)[3]—is one of the best investments in personalizing learning. Ever. **That's a future we can all get behind**.

What More Work in AI Will Make These Teachers All- Powerful?

What do we have to do to bring teachers at the center of technological process to improve teaching and learning? The kind of work that gives them the insight into the student experience and does the heavy lifting of repetitive and laborious tasks, like an overworked TA does. This insight will come, not from opaque and shallow learning technologies which are meant for one-size-fits-all, but through experiments in authentic in-class and out-of-class observations leading to a more complex *modeling* of individual learners and their cognitive, socio-cultural, metacognitive, and affective development. This insight will allow us to focus on deeper differentiation, by taking the whole child into consideration.

These and many more problems and opportunities will not automatically be understood by AI scientists, who, by the nature of their job descriptions, will not be immersed in highly human and messy spaces of human interaction and learning, like classrooms. Some part of the burden is on the educators and learning researchers to express their needs, for the AI community to grapple with, in non-shallow conversations.

Our collective work so far has laid a foundation that will set up, what will look like, "overnight breakthroughs" in the years 2030–2040 or possibly later. Whatever the work to achieve these breakthroughs may be, I believe that it seems inevitable that with our momentum and breadth of literature today, it might not take 40 more years for today's infant AI to build the cognition of a grown-up human. Tenenbaum et al.[4] project that the roadmap for this work will entail making progress in five key verticals: consciousness, meaning, learning, culture, and creativity.[5] This will help us answer some of the key questions we had leapfrogged over when we began the AI journey.

At some point in this journey, we will arrive at an inflection point, which will allow us to vastly reduce the inequalities in teaching and learning capabilities around the world. In our *function* to *maximize* learning outcomes, the *coefficients* to the *variables* "birthplace" and "wealth" will approach 0. Said in other words, at some point in the future, AI, among other things, will help us make the socioeconomic circumstances a child is born into matter less and less in the quest to achieve a high-quality education.

And that is only imaginable if we take an optimistic view of AI in teaching and learning, because it will support us in shaping its design, applications, and research in the years to come.

Notes

1 Tenenbaum et al. (2018). *Building machines that learn & think like people—Prof. Josh Tenenbaum ICML2018*. Retrieved July 15, 2018 from www.youtube.com/watch?v=RB78vRUO6X8.

2 Luckin, R., Holmes, W., Griffiths, M., & Forcier, L. B. (2016). *Intelligence unleashed: An argument for AI in education*. London: UCL Knowledge Lab.
3 An idea made popular by Rose Luckin, UCL Knowledge Lab.
4 Tenenbaum et al. (2018).
5 Tenenbaum et al. (2018). Retrieved February 8, 2018 from www.youtube.com/watch?v=7ROelYvo8f0.

Appendix A: A Short History of AI For Improving Teaching and Learning

> This piece is almost entirely a simplistic review, commentary, and summary of a well-documented history of the interplay between AI and teaching and learning titled "The Intertwined Histories of Artificial Intelligence and Education" by Shayan Doroudi. The research and synthesis are either entirely Prof. Doroudi's or by the individuals mentioned in this summary. I am a mere commentator here. This history begins circa 1956, with references to work going as far back as the late 1800s, and ends circa 2000. The work in the past two decades is considered contemporary, and thus beyond the scope of this piece. Note that the sequence of discussions below is not in the order of the timeline.

The discipline at the intersection of AI and teaching and learning is relatively nascent when we take a long-term historical perspective. Its history is based mostly on the people who spent time on it in academic settings, and their ideas, contributions, and early results. The key people involved in the history that we will be discussing are:

Marvin Minsky *Early founder of AI, cognitive scientist*	Herbert Simon and Allen Newell *Early founders of AI*
John R. Anderson *An inventor of ITSs*	Seymour Papert *Pioneer of constructionist movement*
Jean Piaget *Inventor of constructivism*	John Dewey *Psychologist and education reformer*
Roger Schank *NLP and Learning Sciences pioneer*	Andrea diSessa *Inventor of "knowledge in pieces"*

This is unlike the history of a practice, like jazz music, or the history of human development or progress, like the building of ancient cities. The history of AI and teaching and learning has primarily been a scientific endeavor with a lot of quests for theory generation and experimentation, similar to attempts to build a better understanding of outer space. **I say "primarily" instead of "entirely" because teaching and learning isn't entirely a perfect scientific process now, is it?** The answer to this question has puzzled many for the entirety of this journey. And it has shaped the different ways of thinking about the interplay between AI and teaching and learning. Unlike other scientific inventions, it isn't a thing that can be invented, making it either exist or not exist at a moment in time, like the light bulb, the telephone, the airplane, etc. It's a little more complicated; it's one of those "the journey is the destination" kind, but without the unnecessary spiritual philosophy.

To understand this interplay, for a brief period that lasts the next few pages, put aside your existing notions of AI and teaching and learning and come with me to discover a new outlook.

Uncovering the Mysteries of the Human Mind

If you set aside the differences in opinions of people working in your school, the challenges of fair representation and clashing agendas, and the range of hurdles of administrative chores including scheduling, paperwork, and reporting, at the end of the day, the primary purpose of schooling, and specifically your presence in that ecosystem, is to improve and deliver student learning through teaching. **And a requisite for teaching is having a better understanding of the minds of students and the opportunity to create more deeper learning moments**. You may not think of your job to be this; you might say "but I just teach languages." But, in practice, you are working on each of those student's minds when you teach. Better teachers are better at understanding and harnessing the opportunities of those minds, and not-so-good teachers are, well, not-so-good at it.

But the administrative pressures and pace of schools do not allow for disciplined deeper dives into how students are learning. They also don't offer bigger insights into teaching differently. Student performance numbers reveal how much pressure we need to exert, but do not tell us how to do things differently. And so, we depend on external experts to train us in how students might be learning, or what new strategies are known to teach differently, so they engage more and learn faster. These experts rely on two things: **(1) evidence from practice and experience**, and **(2) science and experimentation**. If you open any book or go to any conference on teaching and learning, the advice offered will rely on one of these two things. That said, I want to acknowledge that yes, this expertise does not always work well.

But one common theme among good experts is that they are interested in understanding and improving these processes of student minds, more formally known as **cognition**. As it turns out, many of the key individuals who made pioneering progress in the early days of AI were people who used science and experimentation to understand human cognition. Thereby, being **cognitive scientists**. Yes, they were interested in the very same things educators were, and have always been, interested in: How do humans learn? How do humans process new knowledge? How do humans reason? How is expertise acquired?

The only point of difference between these scientists and educators is that these AI people were consequently interested in how machines could think. Why machines, though? Here is where philosophies and objectives diverged. While many saw the study of teaching machines to think as an opportunity to better model and understand how humans think and to eventually improve human learning, others were driven by how machines could be improved for the purpose of assisting humans perform tasks. Both were noble endeavors, but we will focus on the former group of people and their work, because these were scientists working primarily for human learning. They were interested in what you and I are interested in.

The Two Different Ways of Working With Machines

Now, these people, the ones we said were interested in understanding how humans think to consequently improve human learning, had two paths towards studying the interplay between machines and human cognition.

The first was what you are probably thinking of: **having machines interact with humans to help humans learn faster and better**. This was either done by "[simulating] human cognition"[1]—a way of saying machines building an understanding of where the human's mind is at—to offer the best ways to learn more **or** by giving them an environment and objects to create and explore worlds with.

Simulating human cognition was pioneered by John R. Anderson, who used a theory called **Adaptive Control of Thought—Rational** (ACT-R) and later a technique called **Bayesian Knowledge Tracing** (BKT) to create **Intelligent Tutoring Systems** (ITSs), something introduced and discussed in the book. We will get to the key underpinning of ACT-R theory very soon, but the broad gist of BKT and ITSs is that once a machine could understand where a student's mind is at, it can guide the student in his/her learning journey and keep improving the machine's understanding of the student's cognition.

But there were also cognitive scientists like Seymour Papert and Marvin Minsky, who together worked on a bottom-up general theory of intelligence that outlined that the mind is like a society of independent agents. Papert took his mentor Jean Piaget's ideas of **constructivism** and came up with the theory of **constructionism. While** *constructivism* **is limited to explaining a student's experiences with the world in general,** *constructionism* revolved around the ideas that "student's (cognitive) constructions are best supported by having objects (whether real or digital) to build and tinker with."[2] He believed that students' interactions with computers could fundamentally alter and improve how children learn and were seen at the time as invariable series of development stages of the human mind. Incidentally, Papert's ideas of *constructionism* manifested themselves in the form of his invention of the programming language for kids called LOGO.

The second way of working with machines, which actually began earlier, was **teaching machines to think and perform tasks like humans, to try to discover more optimal ways of learning from how machines behave**. This was pioneered by the two professors Herbert Simon and Allen Newell, who created a **symbolic** program called the "Logic Theorist" to prove mathematical theorems. A *symbolic* program attempts to make a machine use logic, similar to what a human mind might use to perform a task, representing reasoning and knowledge in symbols instead of statistical equations. Think about it as a computer program emulating the same steps as a student would use to answer a mathematics exercise. Since one of the goals was to understand how human minds learn and process information, the result was the birth of a branch of psychology called **information-processing psychology**. But Simon and Newell weren't just interested in any human mind, they were specifically interested in how the minds of experts learned and processed information. This is unlike Papert and Minsky, who were interested in the minds of children. Unsurprisingly, since *Intelligent Tutoring Systems* were designed to allow anyone, and not just young children, to learn with the support of machines, the *ACT-R theory* used in *Intelligent Tutoring Systems* was based on this idea of *information-processing psychology*.

There was another strategy in teaching machines to think and perform tasks like humans, which resulted from the thinking that machines can be made to think like the biological make-up of the human mind: one that involves emulating neural networks of the brain. This originally came to be known as **connectionism** and was a predecessor to modern **deep learning**, discussed in depth in this book.

The Two Ends of Studying Cognition and Learning

Remember how earlier in this piece I left a dangling question about how scientific teaching and learning were? This question keeps coming back and is at the root of the two ends of studying cognition and learning. And it was first formalized in the 1970s by a cognitive scientist named Roger Schank. More specifically, if you believe more strongly that there is a clear and measurable scientific explanation and structure for everything in the process of learning, you are closer to the **neat** end of this spectrum. If, on the other hand, you align with a less elegant scientific explanation around learning, in that student learning cannot be crafted through perfectly scientific rules and that there are many forces interacting in ways hard to codify to create learning opportunities, you are closer to the **scruffy** end of the spectrum. Both ends have some very smart proponents and theories to justify their positions, leaving this less of a debate and more of a state of perspectives.

At the *neat* end of the spectrum were people like Simon, Newell, and Anderson, who advocated for the need to develop a science of education, comparing it to how medicine was based on a deep knowledge of biological sciences, and the practice of engineering on modern physics and chemistry. They saw the opportunity for a similar science of psychology. They were highly critical of "arbitrary measures"[3] of teaching, which they compared to doctrines of folk medicine. I imagine that you have also pondered, at some point or other, if there was any logical basis for how children are taught. Logic—right—logic is what they were big proponents of; that there are logical procedures and rules in doing something, as described in the *information-processing psychology*. They gravitated towards the idea that learning is about acquiring knowledge, and that cognition could be studied and programmed or taught to computers, scientifically. This would allow computers to do human-like work in helping or teaching humans.

And there was also Noam Chomsky, the famous linguist, who focused on the syntax and grammar of language. Which had clear rules, thereby putting him closer to the *neat* end of the spectrum. Roger Schank noted that Chomsky believed that "the mind should behave according to certain organized principles,"[4] which Schank did not believe was the case. This leads us to the other end of the spectrum.

On the other end of the spectrum, the **scruffy** end, were also a lot of cognitive scientists, but with more nuanced and less elegant mathematical theories for learning. Such new educational theories that arose in the 1990s on the *scruffy* end were less information-centric, and more human-centric. Among them was the highly popular **situated cognition**, advocated by scholars John Seely Brown and Allan Collins, which argued that "knowledge is situated, being in part a product of the activity, context, and culture in which it is developed and used."[5] This, in a sense, dismissed the notion that there could be perfectly replicable universal rules that govern the learning process. And then there was Jean Piaget's famous theory of *constructivism*, the theory on which Papert's *constructionism* (different spellings) was based.

At the heart of Piaget's theory of *constructivism* is the idea that "knowledge and the world are both constructed and constantly reconstructed through personal experience"[6] of children. Pay extra attention to the phrase "through personal experience"; this wasn't generic knowledge where the logic was the same across all children. It was personal and experiential.

Papert and Minsky, although students of *neat* scientific approaches earlier in their careers, found themselves aligning to ideas on the *scruffy* end too. As a result, they wanted to create a general theory that explained intelligence both in children and in machines. Note again, they were interested in intelligence in children, and not high-performing experts. At the heart of their theory was the idea that there are a number of small individually unsophisticated pieces in the mind that have their own independent way of reasoning, but when they come together, they form intelligence. They called these "micro-worlds." They formed "[a] society of mind," Minsky wrote in 1988,[7] and the connections between these could learn to do complex tasks.

Researcher Andrea diSessa advanced this idea with his own theory, called "Knowledge in Pieces," in 1988.[8] diSessa argued that the pieces (he called them "p-prims") provide explanations for phenomena like: "increased effort begets greater results; the world is full of competing influences for which the greater 'gets its way,' even if accidental or natural 'balance' sometimes exists," etc. And that these pieces could individually be activated when a situation or task demanded them to be.

Schank, like Chomsky, was immersed in understanding language and the role it played. But unlike Chomsky, he was focused on the nuance of the semantics of language, thereby landing closer to the *scruffier* end. He saw a need for people to see understanding intelligence more like how a biologist looks at the world, and less how a physicist does. In his words,

> [t]he biologist's philosophy of science says that human beings are what they are, you find what you find, you

try to understand it, categorize it, name it, and organize it. If you build a model and it doesn't work quite right, you have to fix it. It's much more of a "*discovery*" view of the world.

Reconciling History to Make Progress

Does a more scientific lens lend itself to a more significant opportunity for thinking about the role of artificial intelligence in teaching and learning? Or do the *scruffier* hard-to-mathematically-prove theories give us a better opportunity for doing the same? Fortunately for us, the right question to grapple over is not an either–or question.

As you will infer from arguments and examples in the rest of this book, while mathematical techniques give us many means to measure and understand some kinds of cognition and grow them, both lenses play a very important role in helping us determine where, and to what extent, machines should be involved in the teaching and learning process; and where humans perform better than machines, regardless of how *neat* or *scruffy* the context might be. Interestingly, modern AI, specifically machine learning, is an amalgamation of a *scruffy* theory applied in mathematically elegant ways. That is because it tries to find patterns from messy datasets, rather than following any neatly defined rules. And modern teaching and learning research (without the use of technology) is *neater*, while its implementation is often *scruffier*. One can make such an argument because every question in such research is often studied in very controlled classroom settings with finely articulated research methods, while the instructional practice guidelines that emerge from such findings are often vague in trying to adapt to schools with different educational models, structures, and alignments.

We may choose to resort to this reconciliation in advice from the seventh most-cited article in the *Educational Researcher* by Anna Sfard in 1998, titled "On two metaphors for learning and the dangers of choosing just one."[9] Sfard argues that there are two dominant metaphors used in describing learning: the acquisitionist metaphor (i.e., that learning is acquiring knowledge) and the participationist metaphor (i.e., that learning is the process of becoming a participant in a community), and argues that while most researchers accept one, we must accept both. The acquisitionist metaphor is aligned to the *neat* end, while the participationist one is aligned to the *scruffy* end.

As many of us indeed accept both, and give due credit to the theorists of by-gone eras, we may humbly and optimistically yield that the best of AI in teaching and learning is ahead of us, and that we don't yet fully know the power, validity, and efficacy of either of these lenses.

Notes

1 Anderson, J. R., Boyle, C. F., & Reiser, B. J. (1985). Intelligent tutoring systems. *Science*, 228, 456+. Retrieved from https://link.gale.com/apps/doc/A3742489/AONE?u=sacr16736&sid=AONE&xid=f662b47c.
2 Doroudi, S. (2019). *The intertwined histories of Artificial Intelligence and education (Draft)*.
3 Dewey, J. (1900). Psychology and social practice. *Psychological Review*, 7(2), 105.
4 Brockman, J. (1996). *Third culture*. Touchstone: Simon & Schuster (Trade Division).
5 Brown, J. S., Collins, A., & Duguid, P. (1989). Situated cognition and the culture of learning. *Educational Researcher*, 18(1), 32–42. Retrieved from https://doi.org/10.2307/1176008.
6 Ackermann, E. (2001). Piaget's Constructivism, Papert's Constructionism: What's the difference? *Conference Proceedings: In Constructivism: Uses and Perspectives in Education, Volumes 1 & 2* (pp. 85–94). Geneva: Research Center in Education.
7 Minsky, M. (1988). *Society of mind*. New York: Simon and Schuster.

8 DiSessa, A. A. (1988). Knowledge in pieces. In G. Forman & P. B. Pufall (Eds.), *Constructivism in the computer age*. Mahwah, NJ: Lawrence Erlbaum Associates, Inc., 49–70.
9 Sfard, A. (1998). On two metaphors for learning and the dangers of choosing just one. *Educational Researcher*, 27(2), 4–13. Retrieved from https://doi.org/10.2307/1176193.

Appendix B: Common Natural Things Turned to Mathematical Data

When we discuss teaching and learning with data in the same conversation, the picture that most likely forms in your head is that of a gradebook or report card. Or maybe you think of a grid of numbers on how students responded to different questions of an assessment or set of online exercises, or a roster of students with enrollment and attendance data.

But when we consider the broad range of possibilities that AI opens up by doing *pattern recognition*, our notion of what computers can capture goes beyond simple tallied scores and administrative notes. Computers can capture data from "natural" things in the classroom and other surroundings that hasn't been historically captured to run *predictions* on.

Below is a list of how common natural things discussed throughout the book are turned into mathematical data, that computers can understand, for scientists to build better AI with.

Pictures

In Chapter 2, "Feedback and Scoring," we discussed pictures taken of student writing and how we can turn letters and, as a result, words into pictures which are then turned into pixel *matrices*.

Pixel *tensors* (*matrices* of any dimension) are the best way to store still pictures into data. While we discussed black and white images, to turn color pictures into data, instead of storing just one number for each pixel, you can store four numbers: red, blue, green, and alpha for transparency for each pixel. Such pixels could be stored in a higher-dimensional *tensor* than 2-D. We could use one dimension for each of the four attributes that make

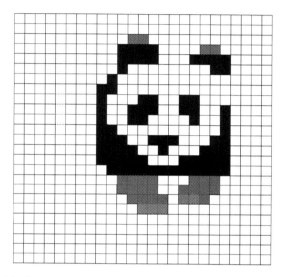

FIGURE B.1 A black and white image of a panda, seen as a composition of pixels

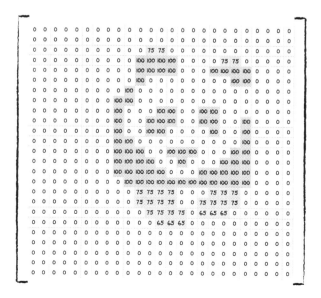

FIGURE B.2 A black and white image of a panda, represented as a mathematical matrix of levels of black and white

up a color. Making it 3-D for one dimension for attributes of the color, and two dimensions for the position x-axis and y-axis.

But even non-handwritten text can be turned into pixels. Pictures of faces, rooms, objects, interactions, etc. can all be turned into pixel-based *tensors* the exact same way as we did for text. Figures B.1 and B.2 are refreshers of what this might look like in practice.

Text

Text is at the heart of most learning in the world. Not only is it the form in which most knowledge, including the factual, creative, and the argumentative kind, resides, but it's also how students express understanding and how we get a sneak peek into their minds.

Unlike other "natural things," once text is in digital form—the kind you can put inside your favorite word processor—it is already a form of mathematical data that is friendly for AI. While this is increasingly true for most text generated in the world today, the reality is that in classrooms around the world, the bulk of the text produced is handwriting. Which is why we discussed what it takes to *predict* handwriting to create digital text in an early chapter in the book.

That said, in applications of AI, depending on the specific purpose, this digital text is transformed into secondary forms which are friendlier to statistical algorithms. Here are a few common scenarios[1]:

Parse Syntax of Statements

Applications which depend on finding key parts of a sentence, or identify errors based on some algorithm, often depend on understanding their syntactic structures. These structures are called **parse trees**, and they can often be generated through algorithms that read and dissect sentences. For example, they look like this, when visualized for the sentence "Pingwei met Rohini":

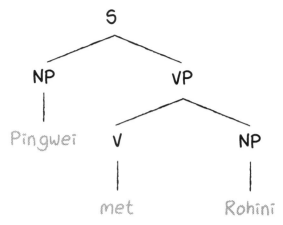

FIGURE B.3 A parse tree

Here, S stands for sentence, NP for noun phrase, VP for verb phrase, and V for verb.

Build Vectors From Tokens

Many applications around making *predictions* with text involve organizing or retrieving the most relevant text for an intended purpose. This always begins with "tokenizing" and "normalizing" text into *n-grams* (introduced in Chapter 7, "Deeper, Higher-order, Authentic Learning")—which means splitting the words in sentences and often removing filler words, removing punctuation, and stripping words to their root forms (so "walks" and "walked" are both counted as "walk," for example).

Then, they can be turned into *vectorized* data using one of the following:

1. *TF-IDF*, a method for associating tokens to texts where the word is most relevant. Discussed in context in Chapter 7, "Deeper, Higher-order, Authentic Learning."
2. *Bag-of-words*, a method for associating words with how commonly they show up. Discussed in context in Chapter 6, "Curriculum Development and Alignment."

3. *word2vec* (or **GloVe**): methods for associating likely similar words with each other, especially coming from sequences, like in a sentence. *word2vec* is introduced in context in Chapter 8, "Teacher Education and Professional Development."

Having text as lots of *vectors* allows the creation of *neural network models* that use text to make *predictions* around meaning, translation, connection to other text, knowledge extraction, making connections with images, etc.

Applications Associated With Speech

One area where computers may need to turn text into mathematical data slightly differently is in the case of applications of speech, that is, when text is being turned into speech audio or speech is being turned into text. In these cases, instead of *predicting* words and syntactical structures, the focus is on predicting sounds.

And so, the process often begins with turning the text into chunks of sounds. This is done at the "grapheme" level (short continuous sounds, like syllables). Each of these graphemes may be represented as its audio counterpart known as a phoneme, which can be turned in speech data, as covered in the next section.

Speech

Recording and analyzing both teacher and student speech offers enormous opportunities for supporting better teaching and learning, as covered in several chapters. Additionally, a large amount of material meant for listening, especially in second-language acquisition, can be better understood to support teacher choice of materials.

Unlike the way of preparing statistically friendly data from pictures as pixels that can directly be used in AI applications, speech has been a little more complicated.

It might be interesting to know that today's newest and most advanced techniques use the raw waveform audio file (yep, the one that opens on Spotify or VLC Player) as the data to start off with.

Then, historically, *feature engineering* (something discussed in the Chapter 6, "Curriculum Development and Alignment") has been used based on what needs to be *predicted* in speech; requiring turning raw waveform audio into some intermediate data to work with.[2] This always begins with the question: how much audio detail will we need for it to be understood and produced? This is captured with something called sample rate.

Then, it is turned into a form of mathematical data called a **log-mel spectrogram**. It is big phrase, but a simple idea. First, let's see what it looks like in Figure B.4.[3]

This is hardly informative! Even a color version would hardly be better. Let's try an explanation in words. Unlike those 2-D waves you are used to seeing when the levels of audio are sometimes visualized, a *log-mel spectrogram* is a multi-dimensional representation of the frequencies along the duration of the

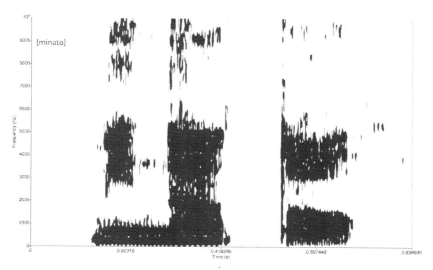

FIGURE B.4 Black and white version of a "spectrogram," from Wiktionary

audio, which takes into account that maximum and minimum set of frequencies that humans can hear. These *log-mel spectrograms* can easily be stored as *vectors*.

Video

Footage of instruction in action is an excellent source of insight for teacher training. On the student side, performance footage of playing a sport, a recital or presentation, a theatrical show, and a conversation are all sources of potential media to run *predictions* on, to get better insights in student ability.

At the end of the day, video is nothing but many pictures changing at a frequent pace, along with audio. So, the video data is essentially a combination of lots of picture data. So, there is nothing special with how to represent it for computers to understand other than how pictures are represented. And audio follows the same ways of forming into mathematical data, as discussed in the section on speech.

The only point to remember is that in storing video, one needs to determine the sample rate, just like in the case of speech. And in some cases of *prediction*-making, the sampling on the audio and the images in the video should be the same.

Knowledge

Throughout the book, we discuss different forms of knowledge and how they facilitate curriculum, instruction, and assessment decision-making in the context of artificial intelligence.

At their most basic form, each piece of knowledge is expressed primarily by text or sometimes even by media like images, audio, and video. And therefore, it is represented as mathematical data expressed by some of the means above. However, that works if we want to use them in isolation. Their real meaning and power come from being organized in higher forms. Key advancements in organizing knowledge that impact how they may be stored and retrieved by computers include:

- **Relational databases**: These are the original and most popular kind of databases where a property of a piece of knowledge can be tied to one or more shared attributes. These are introduced in Chapter 4, "Empowering Students with Physical and Learning Challenges."
- **Graph databases**: In these databases, a series of pieces of knowledge could be associated with each other through connections which are descriptive. These pieces of knowledge could then be fetched based on their connections. These are often used to store *knowledge graphs*, a topic discussed in Chapter 4, "Empowering Students with Physical and Learning Challenges."
- **Object storage**: A paradigm in storing data that organizes data as things which have some structured meaning, as opposed to "files," which is the way computers have traditionally stored knowledge.

While there are many such technological advancements, they are only useful when "modeled" the right way. Modeling is a systematic process of understanding the relationship of what knowledge is stored and how it is intended to be used, to the underlying technology. How it is intended to be used, a topic called **knowledge retrieval**, is a whole other area of technological progress closely tied to the technologies listed above.

3-D space

Pictures and videos are considered some of the best sources of information to describe a scene or object. But if you think about it, pictures are only what a scene or object is from one angle, and videos extend that one angle limitation to many points of time. So, while this tells us a lot about a space, it doesn't tell us everything at all times. Additionally, 2-D pictures are limited in what they can tell us, and the cameras are limited in what they can record.

In several industrial applications, historically, an alternative to using camera imagery to understand spaces, especially those inaccessible to cameras, has been to use radars based on sound (as in SONAR) and light or heat (as in laser-based LiDAR). These generate something called **point clouds**, or x, y, and z coordinates of objects and spaces, thereby having three dimensions. They don't capture pictures of the space from each of these dimensions, but are useful in applications where detection of objects and their positions is valuable. Here is what a point cloud of a space may look like in Figure B.5[4]:

While there are not many known applications for use of understanding of all dimensions of a space to improve teaching and learning, it isn't entirely unlikely that people will have better ideas involving the entirety of space as we advance in *screen-less* AI inside classrooms.

FIGURE B.5 3-D point cloud from an iPhone LiDAR inside of a subway

Vitals

Another set of data that might seem distant today but might potentially find a novel non-intrusive application in the future is understanding the well-being of an individual through his or her vitals. Some of the applications of capturing these vitals are popular in modern culture in the form of wristbands connected to phones. Regardless of how they are captured, and ideally without eroding the privacy of children, these may be used to the extent that they help a teacher understand a student's health and alertness at any given point in time without needing students to gather the courage to vocalize it or fearing embarrassment for seeming disingenuous.

The scope of the variety of data (pulse, speed, movement, altitude, EKG, temperature, perspiration, etc.) is large, so the key idea to remember is that there can be many sensors inside a tracker that can be attached to human skin to capture different kinds of data. And that these sensors can either produce data as simple numbers (mathematically sometimes called **scalars**) or multi-dimensional data stored as *tensors*, in a **time-series** (over a recorded series of time, with known intervals or time at occurrences).

We might also discuss a new type of visceral insight about a person's state, which is becoming less and less far-fetched. We are coming closer and closer to realizing a brain–computer link, possible due to advancements in nano-sensors embedded directly in the brain. Understanding the signals in a human brain at that level of precision may solve a lot of unsolved mysteries about how the human brain learns.

While we may have figured out how to use sensors and computer tools to capture and represent many common natural things around us, we are still in the early stages of figuring out systems to unify and share common language about how we perceive, group, archive, and share our natural world in data. Fortunately, reaching that consensus doesn't stop us from making strides in AI, given a shared global human curiosity to unpack the mysteries of the world.

Notes

1 Grzegorczyk, K. (2019). Vector representations of text data in deep learning. Retrieved from http://arxiv.org/abs/1901.01695.
2 Purwins, H., Li, B., Virtanen, T., Schlüter, J., Chang, S.-Y., & Sainath, T. (2019). Deep learning for audio signal processing. *IEEE Journal of Selected Topics in Signal Processing*, 13(2), 206–219.
3 Spectrogram—*Wiktionary* (n.d.). Retrieved May 20, 2021 from: https://en.wiktionary.org/wiki/spectrogram.
4 Denoyel, A. (2020). *Subway train car—Point cloud version* [Digital]. Retrieved from https://sketchfab.com/3d-models/subway-train-car-point-cloud-version-cc1d9f99f3584fa1a662c3c2154e9fd4.

Index

3-D space 226–7

Abstract Meaning Representation (AMR) 128–9
abstraction 126, 127, 128
Accelerated Reader Bookfinder 132
accuracy 36, 99, 115, 182–3
acoustic features 97
actions 154, 155, 157, 174
activity recognition 98, 173
Adaptive Content Selection 122, 123
Adaptive Control of Thought–Rational (ACT–R) 210, 212
Additive Factors Model 123
affect detection 99, 159, 173
Affectiva 100
affects 99, 100
agents 154, 155
AI xvii; breakthroughs 2, 8; common concerns xxvi; future 203–5; getting started 191–201; history of 207–16; limitations xxiii, 2–3, 30; mathematical vs non-mathematical 6–8; potential xviii, xx, xxviii, 1
AI Complete problems 29
ALEKS 122
Alexa 44
Algorithmia 129
Allen Institute for AI 136
Amazon 44; Mechanical Turk 158; Polly 80
Anderson, John R. 210, 212
Apple 44
Application Programming Interface (API) 198
argument mining 137
articulation 95
Artificial General Intelligence (AGI) 88–9

Artificial Intelligence *see* AI
assessment for learning 124, 135–8
assignments 60
assistive reading devices 79
"at-risk" students 54, 56, 59, 62
attention 42, 63
audio chunks 39
authentic learning 147, 148; *see also* deeper learning
authenticity 158, 160–1
Automatic Essay Scoring 47
automatic question generators 87
Automatic Speech Recognition (ASR) 38, 42, 65, 74, 78, 83, 94–5, 97, 103, 173, 179
autonomy 158, 159–60

backpropagation 40
bag-of-words 133, 170, 222
Baidu 66
Bayes Theorem 101, 102
Bayesian Knowledge Tracing (BKT) 121, 210
behavior management 93–100; deep learning 95, 96, 98, 103; prediction 94, 95, 96, 97, 98, 99, 100, 101, 102, 103, 104, 105, 106, 108
Behavior Signals 97
bias 20, 56, 99
Bing Entity Search 86
Bloom, Benjamin 122, 149
Bloom's taxonomy 149–50, 151
brain areas 55
Brown, John Seely 213
buggy rules 167, 168

calculus 41
Carnegie Learning 122
CCTV footage 98

Central Processing Units (CPUs) 194–5
challenges 177–8, 188–9; accuracy 182–3; domain-specific research 184–8; lack of enough data 178–81
Chomsky, Noam 213, 214
Clarifai 98
classes 58, 80, 83
classification 55, 56, 58, 59, 60, 74, 98, 99, 187
classroom management 93–110; deep learning 95, 96, 98, 103; prediction 94, 95, 96, 97, 98, 99, 100, 101, 102, 103, 104, 105, 106, 108
classroom observations 172
cloned voice 87
clustering 60, 61, 133, 137–8, 152, 169
coefficients 12, 13, 17, 19, 20, 21, 23, 32, 40, 42, 81, 205
cognition 2, 3, 30, 209, 212–15
cognitive scientists 209, 212
Cognitive Tutor 122
collaboration 158, 160
collaborative filtering 159, 172
college readiness 53, 66; "at-risk" students 54, 56, 59, 62
Collins, Allan 213
common sense understanding 136
Common Voice 179
competencies 118–21, 122, 123, 131, 153, 160–1, 168, 173
complex problem spaces xxv
compound sentences 10
computation cost 194–5
competitions 201
Computer Vision 97–8, 99
conferences 200–1
connectionism 212
constructionism 211, 213
constructivism 211, 213–14
consumable knowledge 124, 125–34, 135
context 41–2
conversational models 84
Convolutional Neural Networks (CNNs) 35–6, 38, 44, 74, 99
core knowledge 3

coreference resolution 136
corpus 18
COVID-19 pandemic xiii, xiv, xviii
creative works 131, 132
critical thinking 28
curriculum development 28, 113–14, 166; assessment for learning 124, 135–8; consumable knowledge 124, 125–34, 135; deep learning 121, 126; learning outcomes 116–24; prediction 114, 117, 121, 123, 125, 126, 127, 129, 130, 131, 133, 134; teachable materials 124–38; understanding of content or knowledge 114–16

Danielson, Charlotte 4
Danielson Framework 4
data 17–18, 31; acquisition, preparation, and storage 195; common natural things turned to mathematical data 219–29; labelled 60, 75, 96, 137, 149, 150, 160, 196; lack of 178–81
data-based AI 6, 199
data hunger 17, 24, 37, 45, 55, 80, 87, 102, 120, 137, 152, 158
data mining 107
data needs 196–7
data privacy 196–7
datasets 18, 45, 133, 178, 179, 180
DataShop 179
decision-making 7
decoders 63
Deep Knowledge Tracing 121
Deep Learning 22, 25, 31, 32, 34–5, 36, 37, 38, 40, 43, 63, 185, 212; and deeper learning 148, 149; behaviour and classroom management 95, 96, 98, 103; curriculum development 121, 125–6; personalized support 74, 79, 80, 81, 82, 83, 84
deeper learning 147–53; alternative focus for AI 161–2; over a longer period 153–61
dependent clauses 9–10

Descript 43
Dialogue Systems 83, 84, 87
differentiation 41
digital pictures 32; *see also* pixels
discourse 126
discriminators 130
diSessa, Andrea 214
disruptive behaviour 93, 97
domain-specific research 184–8
Doroudi, Shayan 207
Drools 120
Dropbox 32
Duolingo 201
Duolingo English Test 47
Duplex 84
dyslexia 77

e-rater 45
Echo 44
educational data mining 107
Ekman, Paul 96
embeddings 168, 169, 170
emotion 95–100
empowerment 71–90; *see also* personalized support
encoder-decoder 63
English Learners (EL) 48, 62, 66
entities 85, 86, 87, 117, 129
Entity Resolution 85
environments 154, 155, 156
error 41, 160
ethics 105
examinations 28, 53
examples 18
expert models 187–8
expert systems 119–21, 122, 197
experts 186
explainable AI 185
extraction 126–7

Facebook 98
facets 118
facial recognition 98
facial tracking 99
far-field voice recognition 43, 44
feature engineering 132, 133, 134, 224

feature learning 132, 133, 134
features 168
feedback 27, 41
Figure Eight 158
fluency 38
formative assessment 38
formulae 10
FortressIQ 174
Framework for Teaching (FFT) 4
functions 13, 14, 15, 17, 19, 20–1, 34, 37, 39, 40, 42, 57, 58, 59, 60, 185, 205; neural networks 63, 81; stacked functions 22, 23, 32, 35, 36, 39, 40

generalizability 184, 199, 200
Generative Adversarial Networks (GANs) 130
generative modelling 129, 130, 152–3
generators 130
GitHub 199
GloVe 223
Google 44, 61, 66, 198; Creative Lab 58; Duplex 84; Read Along 78
Gradescope 38
grading 29
grammar 37, 45; dependent clauses 9–10
Grammarly 45
graph databases 226
graph representations 135
graphemes 79
Graphics Processing Units (GPUs) 195
graphs 13, 14, 15, 16
Gross, Daniel xxvii, xxviii
group discussions 28

hand gestures 58
handwriting 31, 32, 33, 34, 36, 57, 74, 221
Hidden Markov Model 103, 121, 154
higher-order learning 147; *see also* deeper learning
higher-order questions 28, 29, 44
"Home" 44
HomePod 44

human capital 194
Human-Computer Interaction 162, 185, 193
Human-In-The-Loop (HITL) techniques 157, 162, 186, 197
human-like speech 79, 80

IBM Watson 86, 97
image captioning 75
Imitation Learning 174
in-person learning xviii
"In-Service" professional development 172–4
"inaccuracy gap" 183
inclusive learning environment 66
information extraction 116
information-processing psychology 211, 212, 213
information retrieval 150
innovation 191–201
inputs 19, 20, 32, 34, 39, 40, 41, 42, 55, 60, 63, 98, 102, 123, 126, 159, 180, 187, 199; listening devices 43; personalized support 73, 76, 81; supervised learning 99
Intelligence Augmentation 161
Intelligent Tutoring Systems (ITSs) xxii, 118, 122, 123, 124, 172, 187, 188, 204, 210, 212
IntelliMetric 47
intent parsing 46

K-12 education xxi
Khan Academy 123
knowledge 225–6
knowledge base 85, 86, 87, 116
knowledge components 118
knowledge extraction 116
knowledge graphs 85, 87, 116, 128, 226
knowledge needs 196–7
Knowledge Representation and Reasoning (KRR) 85
knowledge representations 116, 117
knowledge retrieval 226
knowledge tracing 121, 122, 183, 184

labeled data 60, 75, 96, 137, 149, 150, 160, 196
language learning 77–8, 201; *see also* English Learners
language models 37, 46, 64, 75, 97, 134, 199
layers 22, 35, 185
learner models 121
learning analytics 105–8, 123
learning challenges 71–90
learning outcomes 116–24
LearnLab 179
least-invasive technologies xix
line of best fit 13
linear arrays 43
linear regression 13, 15, 16, 17, 20, 23, 55, 61
listening devices 43
log-mel spectrogram 224
logistic regression 55–6, 61, 76, 123
LOGO 211
long short-term memory (LSTM) networks 98
low interpretability 185
lower-order questions 28
Lumilo 123
Lumos 98

Machine Learning (ML) 20, 22, 24–5, 31–2, 37, 40, 45, 55, 60, 76, 78, 98, 99, 100, 103, 126, 129, 130, 134, 154, 155, 157, 158, 168, 180, 181, 183, 185, 197–8, 199, 200, 204
Machine Translation 63, 64, 65, 66
Maluuba 87
Markov Decision Process (MDP) 154, 155
Markov models 102, 154; Hidden Markov Model 103, 121, 154
Massive Open Online Courses (MOOCs) xxii
mastery 123
mastery learning 122
mathematical AI 6–8
mathematical calculations 8–22
mathematical data 219–29
mathematical models 19–20, 21, 24

matrices 33–4, 36, 39, 63, 65, 76, 129, 168; pixels 219
maximization 20, 22, 23, 25, 155, 205
Mechanical Turk 158
memorization 28, 29
meaningful interaction 82
misconception analysis 167, 169
microphones 43, 44, 78
Microsoft: Bing Entity Search 86; Seeing AI 76; Translator 64
minimal AI 194–6
Minsky, Marvin 211, 212, 214
mispronunciation detection and diagnosis 78
model-free reinforcement learning 156
models 19–20, 21, 24, 36, 39, 60, 174, 178, 179, 180, 181, 195, 197–8, 204; classification 58; expert models 187–8; generalizability 199; generative modelling 129, 130, 152–3; Hidden Markov model 103, 121, 154; language models 37, 46, 64, 75, 97, 134, 199; Markov models 102, 103, 154; misconception models 170, 171; multi-speaker models 81; multimodal learning 99; pedagogy model 185; personalized support 79, 81; pre-trained models 199; speech recognition 74; student modeling 121, 157, 182, 183; voice recognition 43
modes 74, 99, 107
Mozilla 179
multi-agent Reinforcement Learning 160
multi-speaker models 81
multimodal learning 99
Multimodal Learning Analytics 106, 186
Mursion 171

n-grams 151, 222
Named Entity Recognition (NER) 85
Natural Language Generation (NLG) 79, 83, 129
Natural Language Processing (NLP) 44–5, 63, 75, 79, 85, 137, 150, 152, 184
Natural Language tools 86
Natural Language Understanding (NLU) 46, 47, 83
near-field voice recognition 43
networks 41; *see also* neural networks
Neural Machine Translation (NMT) 63
neural network functions 98
neural networks 22, 23, 32, 34, 40, 41, 63, 64, 65, 79, 80, 81, 108, 130, 149, 170, 181, 183, 223; Convolutional Neural Networks (CNN) 35–6, 38, 44, 74, 99; deep neural networks 158; Recurrent Neural Networks (RNNs) 39, 40, 42, 43, 44, 63, 74, 98, 102, 121
Newell, Allen 211, 212
Ng, Andrew 2, 178
non-mathematical AI 6–8

object storage 226
one-vs-all 58
Optical Character Recognition (OCR) 31
outputs 19, 20, 35, 39, 40, 57, 58, 60, 81, 171
Overdub 82
overfitting 180

Papert, Seymour 211, 212, 213, 214
paraphrase generation 129
parse trees 221
parsing 46
pattern recognition 3–5, 8, 9, 11, 19, 27, 53, 56, 126, 219; brain areas 55
Pearson 47
pedagogy 185
perception 2, 3, 59
performance tasks 135
personalized support 73; deep learning 74, 79, 80, 81, 82, 83, 84; inputs 73, 76, 81; predictions 73,

74, 75, 76, 79, 80, 81, 83, 84, 85; scaffolding 82; training 79, 81, 82
phonemes 79
physical challenges 71–73, 76, 81–90
Piaget, Jean 211, 213–14
pictures 219–20
pieces of text 127
Pixel Buds 66
pixels 32–3, 219–20
point clouds 227
policies 154, 156, 157, 160
Polly 80
polynomial terms 20
pre-trained models 199
prediction 20, 21, 23, 24, 27, 29, 32, 34, 35, 36, 37, 39, 41, 42, 55, 58, 60, 61, 198, 204, 219; behaviour and classroom management 94, 95, 96, 97, 98, 99, 100, 101, 102, 103, 104, 105, 106, 108; challenges 181, 183, 186, 187; common natural things turned to mathematical data 221, 222, 223, 224, 225; curriculum development 114, 117, 121, 123, 125, 126, 127, 129, 130, 131, 133, 134; deeper learning 149, 150, 151, 152, 153–4, 156, 159, 160; minimal viable AI 194, 195, 196, 199, 201; Natural Language Processing (NLP) 45, 63, 64, 65; personalized support 73, 74, 75, 76, 79, 80, 81, 83, 84, 85; teacher education and development 170, 173, 174; voice recognition 43
privacy 108, 196–7
probability 133
professional development 165, 172–4; *see also* teacher education
project-based learning 28
Project Essay Grade 47

qualitative evaluation 131
quantitative evaluation 131
question-answering systems 87
question generators 87, 135, 136, 138
Quill 45

rate memorization 28, 29
Read Along 78
reading ability 48
reading comprehension 135
reading levels 131–2
real-time awareness tools 123
recommender systems/recommendation systems 159, 172
Recurrent Neural Networks (RNNs) 39, 40, 42, 43, 44, 63, 74, 98, 102, 121
regression 13, 15, 16, 17, 20, 23, 40, 55–6, 60, 61, 76, 123
Reinforcement Learning (RL) 155, 156, 157, 162, 174; multi-agent RL 160
relational databases 86, 226
relevance 158, 159
repetitive tasks 5
representations 116, 134, 185
reverberation 43
rewards 154, 155, 156, 174

scaffolding 82
scalars 228
Schank, Roger 212, 213, 214
scientific community 200–1, 209–15
scores 60
screen-less classrooms xviii, xxiii, 37, 106, 184–6, 227
seeing AI 76
semantic networks 116
sensors/sensory data 2, 18, 31, 75, 97, 108
sensory challenges 74, 76
sentiments 95–100
sequence-to-sequence 63, 64, 79, 83
Sfard, Anna 215–16
shallow learning 148–53; *see also* deeper learning
"shallow" questions 28
Simon, Herbert 211, 212
simultaneous interpretation 64
Simultaneous Machine Translation 65
Siri 44
situated cognition 213
software programs 199
speaker adaptation 81

speaker diarization 95, 173
speaker separation 95
spectrograms 80
speech 223–5
speech emotion recognition 96, 99, 150
speech impairment 81
speech recognition 38, 39, 42, 65, 74, 78
Speech Synthesis 79, 80, 81, 83, 130
spelling 37
spelling mistakes 44, 46
Squirrel AI Learning 122
stacked functions 22, 23, 32, 35, 36, 39, 40
standardized tests 28, 53
Stanford Question Answering Dataset (SQuAD) 136
states 154, 155, 157
student engagement 28
Student Information Systems 59
student models 121, 122, 123, 157, 182, 183
student talk 38, 62
summarization 125, 127–8
supervised learning 60, 96, 99, 126, 133, 149, 150
symbolic programs 211
syntax 45, 46, 221–3; parsing 46

taxonomies 149–50, 151
Teachable Machine 58
teachable materials 124–38
teacher education 165; pre-service programs 166–71
teachers: changing role xv, xxiii; meaningful interaction 82; workload 4–5, 24
TeachFX 95
Teaching Assistants (TAs) 204
technology tyranny xvii
Tenenbaum, J. 205
tensors 219–20, 228
Term Frequency-Inverse Document Frequency (TF-IDF) 151, 152, 222
text 220, 221

text analysis 45
textbook-driven learning 28
TF-IDF 151, 152, 222
time-series 228
tokens 222–3
Tone Analyzer 97
topic discovery 150
topic modeling 127
training 41, 42, 58, 114, 126, 129, 149, 152, 160, 168, 174, 178, 180, 181, 186, 187, 195, 198; activity recognition models 98; Automatic Speed Recognition (ASR) 78; Natural Language Processing models 75; personalized support 79, 81, 82; pre-trained models 199; voice recognition 43, 44
transcripts 44
transfer learning 181, 199
TurnItIn Revision Assistant 47
tutoring systems 181

unsupervised learning 60, 61, 127, 133, 152, 159
user interface 162, 194, 198

variables 12, 13, 14, 21, 23, 42, 57, 58, 205
vectors 168, 222–4
Versant 47
video footage 97, 104, 225
video tracking 98, 108, 173
virtual reality (VR) 171
visual impairments 74, 76
vitals 228–9
"vivo state" 2, 38
voice cloning 81
voice recognition 43, 44

WiFi Translator 66
Wizard of Oz technique 193
word2vec 170, 223
writing style 57

zone of proximal development 82

Printed in the United States
by Baker & Taylor Publisher Services